AF260886

ADVANCE PRAISE FOR
Speaking Our Truths

"The works reflect on the isolation and widespread fears brought about by the simultaneous stresses of Covid-19, social unrest and racist attacks, and the stresses of reintegration into in-person schooling. They also record peers' cruelty and adults' obliviousness... Some writers' activism is inspirational; others inspire simply by holding on, showing optimism and resilience."

~Kirkus Reviews

"This book is an essential read for anyone wanting a glimpse into the minds and hearts of our youth during the pandemic. It is at times heartbreaking but also hopeful. This is what an authentic student voice sounds like."

~Rebecca Cohen, M.S., M.Ed.
Oregon School Counselor of the Year

"As a public school teacher of 28 years, these global scholars left me speechless. This is the manifesto for generations to come. This is the semester course called, *Voices from the Pandemic*. It will arrive, and I would love to teach the course."

~Andrea Nicole Smith-Morgan
Mindful Awareness Academy for Children

Speaking Our Truths

The –Ism Youth Files

Essays, poetry, art, and short graphic novels by youth about mental health and wellness during pandemic times and beyond

A MediaRites Production

MediaRites.org

Table of Contents

Part I
World On Fire

Part II
. . . That Happened

Part III
The Journey Continues

Contributing Youth Authors and Photo Gallery
The -Ism Youth Files Creative Team
Thanks to Supporters
MediaRites Staff/Board
Copyright Notices

Dedicated to the life and memory of

Julian Wehde

a young talent gone too soon
who inspired this project

Foreword

A longtime friend of mine experienced a devastating loss. A youth in her family died. The tragedy was without doubt amplified by the social isolation experienced during the pandemic.

The COVID-19 pandemic will forever leave an indelible milestone for young people in America and around the world. Just as previous generations experienced war traumas and economic depressions, the last few years have created lasting mental health challenges for youth. Suicide and depression rates skyrocketed and percentages of racial attacks and hate crimes against BIPOC peoples rose to an unbelievable height. It became clear: MediaRites must focus our next project to address youth mental health through a new book and podcast project.

Out of forty submissions, a panel of youth and professional writers selected twenty writers not only from Oregon and Washington but from Indiana, Minnesota, Massachusetts, Connecticut and one selection from Kolkata, India. Each writer received an honorarium payment. During the last year, *The –Ism Youth Files* turned into a mentorship project as we worked with writers to polish their work, and for the podcast, I interviewed each one about the motivations behind their writings and the effects of the pandemic. The goal for *The –Ism Youth Files* is to create more awareness for youth mental health and to break the silence that still exists in communities of color.

We hope this collection of personal essays, poetry and graphic novels will be a chronicle of an unprecedented time for youth about life during and after the pandemic, perhaps encouraging more awareness for a taboo subject especially for the BIPOC communities and the lack of resources for

mental health help for youth with disabilities. One thing
rang clear: all of our young writers affirmed they turned to
writing and artistic creativity as a form of comfort and
healing and as a way to speak their truths to gain a more
optimistic window toward their futures.

*A companion mental health resources
toolkit is also available as a free
download at our website:*
mediarites.org

Dmae Lo Roberts
Executive producer, MediaRites
Winter 2023

Introduction
By
Eleanor Gil-Kashiwabara

The COVID-19 pandemic had, and continues to have, a disproportionate impact on our younger generation of children, teens and young adults--especially those youth who identify as Black, Indigenous People of Color (BIPOC) and/or are part of the disability community.

Perhaps one of the most challenging of the struggles faced by young people is that some are less visible. The pandemic has created a global mental health crisis for our youth, including high rates of depression and anxiety, as well as intense feelings of loneliness and isolation. And now as many are transitioning (or trying to transition) away from the "pandemic times" we are looking at an ongoing mental health crisis because of all that has happened. But what exactly happened? Did it really happen? Where do we go from here? And how are our children and young people doing now?

Speaking Our Truths: The –Ism Youth Files grapples with these questions, and more, through the writings of young artists (ages 10-21) from BIPOC and disability communities. As the mental health consultant for The -Ism Youth Files project, I have spent much time reflecting on and considering the works submitted. Quite a few words come to mind as I think about this collection, including *authenticity, vulnerability, powerful, heartbreak, fear, truth-telling, creativity, intersectional, courage, healing, inspiration, strength, knowledge and hope.* It is one thing to read about the mental health impact of the past few years, and it is another to actually *feel* what this means through the glimpse we get into the inner world of young people through their honest writing and creativity. This book is a reminder we are all still hurting and healing, and it is a gift from this group of youth to their peers showing that they are not alone. The message of this book is that through art and connection, there is hope . . . even in the midst of ongoing struggle.

For BIPOC youth in particular, the added element of re-invigorated demands for Black and Brown racial justice (the most in the U.S. since the Civil Rights Era) that were often not paired with meaningful action, and high rates of anti-AAPI hate crimes served to create additional stress and trauma. There is no mental health professional (or research study) that can convey the impact of COVID-19 and racism and other social-environmental identity/issue intersections on BIPOC youth mental health and wellness as eloquently, emotionally and powerfully as these young people have done collectively through their storytelling. Whether you are a youth, a parent or provider, this book will move you, grow your compassion (even if you have a lot of it already), teach you, inspire you and help you.

During these pandemic times, so many young people felt lonely and isolated. This was a common, collective experience yet so many were alone with this condition. The irony of everyone feeling alone in a world where loneliness and isolation were shared by so many is important to note as a widespread circumstance of the pandemic. Opportunities for conversations and connection were lost and the perspective of others who might be in a similar emotional space was not always available. Even if it was available, dialogue was difficult because everything felt insurmountable in this world that was (and still is), literally and figuratively (as noted by one of our youth writers), on fire.

So, what is the path forward? How do we heal and engage with wellness amidst all of the uncertainty in trying to make sense of the recent past and adapt to a new normal? Do we re-define wellness? And what does it mean to heal? Everyone, including providers, are still figuring this out.

While this book doesn't have all of the answers, we are a step closer because of the bravery and lived truths modeled by our youth writers. Here in this book, this gift, they tell us to remove shame . . . to read, feel, listen and to simply BE. And as a result, young readers will hopefully know that they are not alone.

Part I

World On Fire

COVID: We Went Through That S**t

By Journeya

This has been an emotional year.

To say the least.

My dad is a nurse; he doesn't talk about it really. It reminds me of what my grandmother said about her father who fought in World War II. I always thought that kind of trauma would be our great-grandparents' scene.

I don't think people *really* realize we have lived through shared history.

He and I were separated for three months. On my side I breathed shared air within four walls, and on his side his breath was filtered through a P100 respirator mask for twelve hours on end.

He was one of the lucky ones, my mom says. He used his resources well to get that gas mask, and his resources weren't from the hospital he had thrown his life at. I remember the day well, when he sent us a picture of him all decked out in his new gowns. Dressed all the way down in multiple layers of armored cloth of polyester. And all I could conjure was, "This can't be real. Is it?"

I know, on the other side, that man became someone else.

He hides it well, but he spends a lot more time with us now.

Where I don't get the heroic stories of nursing from my dad, I get it from my friend whose mother is also a healthcare worker. She remembers when it first started, her mom said, "Don't worry about it." But then her mother watched all of them die right there, in those hospital beds.

Those three million people . . .

Summer of 2020 Worldwide Deaths: three million. Out of 7.7 billion people. 7.6 billion left. Though it's a small drop, it's a drop nonetheless. Why do I feel like nobody is really, *really,* talking about that? We weren't ready for it.

She said her mother made them as comfortable as she could while she held each of their hands and felt them slip away while they reached for their strangled last breath.

Our parents, nurses, doctors, and surgeons are living *breathing* warriors, troops, and saints, but that sure as hell didn't come without its pains.

And now we live in winter 2022. Five million deaths are now filling the room. I'll scroll through the media and see bodies in the streets from the undeniable power of this new god we breathe.

I'm beginning to hear the weight of the five million spiraling up. My friends have it now, and that's a lot to process even in itself. It's a daunting game of waiting every day, for someone you love to get it and then have your whole world get choked out. Now just breathing makes all my insides feel twisted inside out.

What a strange world to grow up in. What a strange world to find hope in. What a strange reality where you are terrified of yourself.

COVID 19: "The Virus Who Decides Your Death Date." The product of Pandora's box, it floods through the earth and breaks us in its oh so many ways.

I hurt for the one who released the creature from its cage.

We are not okay, but we are trying to look in this box for a fresh burst of air every single day.

~

Author's Note: This story took form throughout many different timelines of my life. Reading this back to myself, I can pinpoint where I was in my life when I wrote the Before, where I was when I wrote After, and how I felt when I was writing now. In this way the story itself gives me a gift. A gift I plan on showing to my descendants when they ask, "what was your teenage experience?" I hope as the years go on I can look back on this story and see how much my description of my school experienced has changed. I hope this story will begin drawing in people who have had similar stories that need validation. I hope it opens the eyes of many.

THE SAFE PLACE

A free phone app geared towards people of the Black community to provide awareness, education, and hope to African American mental health.

The Evolution

By Adrija Jana

Visiting my grandmother in the summer was a yearly ritual which didn't happen. Instead, I experienced the first-ever "Janta Curfew" (a lockdown of the entire population of India with 1.38 billion people). We had been getting continual news of the dire situation in China, but no one had expected the virus to travel so soon to India. When the lockdown first began, it was a crucial time for students in India because we were taking final exams, and the Grade 12 students were preparing for college. Suddenly, everything came to a standstill, and people who might have been preparing to attend a concert found themselves being asked by the government to bang utensils on their terrace to encourage the front line COVID workers.

After cleaning out every cupboard at home and ensuring there wasn't even a speck of dust at any spot, I sat clueless at home for more than two weeks, not allowed to go out, not even to go up to the terrace, and slowly got bored of binge-watching movies. In India school students take national level board exams twice--once in Grade 10 and again in Grade 12. These two groups of students are called "Board Batches," and the 2020 batch, which I was a part of, will evermore be known as "The COVID Batch." I then came to know of a new app called Zoom.

Everything was online so you could submit assignments late in the evening and sit for school wearing your school shirt and pyjamas. But missing was the chance to walk up to the teacher to ask her something. Nor could you whisper something humorous to your friend sitting beside you. There were countless complaints every day about all the fights happening at someone's place that could be heard mistakenly "unmuting" at the wrong time, or how, when the teacher screen shared a document, showing only colourful scribbles instead of the text.

After a Zoom session as an audience member for my first-ever e-play (online theatre) I started to discover an entirely new side of myself.

I decided to join a theatre workshop organised by the same NGO which had produced the theatre show as a fundraiser for COVID-19 victims. After the workshop, the founder of the NGO asked me to stay back and work for them. I agreed, and that was how I played an active role in helping stranded people in the Sundarbans, a cluster of islands home to mangrove forests filled with globally endangered species. A cyclone struck that area in West Bengal in May 2020.

I went on to organise my first-ever online event—a webinar with eleven prominent panelists, talking about cyber crime and cyber safety. Since then, I have planned and created more than thirty online events for thirty-five different organisations, including a youth group and an international magazine.

Yet I had my fair share of downs. During the first wave of COVID the furious Amphan cyclone ravaged coastal India. It washed away my family's fishery business. This was a huge financial loss for us.

We were still getting used to the idea of the pandemic and lockdown, and there were many rumours on social media. Day after day there were people claiming to be doctors suggesting miracle cures which turned out to be fake. This coupled with many incidents of cybercrime, of which even I was a victim. Without my knowledge, my personal Whatsapp number had been shared on an adult Instagram page. Male strangers sent me unsolicited messages and pictures. I felt panicked, confused and afraid. I could not gather the courage to tell anyone.

Indian society is still to see all genders on an equal level, and the first person to be blamed for this would be me.

This affected my confidence in classes. Logistics are my forte, but I was a Grade 11 student and my opinion was often not valued at some workplaces. At one meeting I remember we were discussing ways to improve social media outreach. I unmuted myself and offered a suggestion. No one responded to it. They carried on with the discussion, ignoring what I had said. The looks they gave me clearly said, "What does a little girl like you understand? Just sit quietly and listen." I felt insignificant and invisible. It would be a long while before I could build my confidence back again, bit by bit.

I had been sheltered and protected by my parents in all ways, and when I was suddenly given a virtual taste of the real world, I found it difficult to cope. In this competition of trying to take the highest credit and get the most appreciation, I felt like I was getting lost. I realised if you wanted to be recognised for what you did, you had to fight for it. What I had initially started to be able to give back to society, became a rat race for self-promotion. That was not me. I valued relations, and not this fight of pushing each other down to rise up. I felt in my heart a lingering sense of unhappiness.

For months, I would be sitting eighteen to twenty hours in front of the mobile phone or laptop screen, trying to balance studies and work with no leisure time. One day I was unable to look at the phone screen without my eyes burning terribly. The doctor said that I was down with a high fever because of "Zoom Fatigue." No one who heard this would believe it was even a thing. I was bedridden for days. and I realised I had not a single moment of "me time" for months. I had simply been working like a robot, following the same routine day after day, until a point when

I didn't even have to know what I was doing to complete a task. When I could finally take some time out to meet my grandmother, it had been ten months since I had last seen her.

In the beginning, the lockdown coupled with the worsening COVID-19 statistics, and the continuous inflow of bad news, seemed to be bearing down on me, and I would be stressed out all the time. There seemed to be negativity wherever I looked. But slowly I learnt to look for the silver lining, weed out the harmful, rejoice in the small moments of happiness and accept and deal with the cloudy periods of despair. And I did need to put my needs before others. If I did take a day off, the world wouldn't turn upside down.

My personal growth through the lockdown was very rewarding. But the pandemic has been a time of intense mental and emotional turmoil for most people. February to May 2021 was especially difficult for me.

Towards the end of January, my grandmother slipped in the washroom and fractured her right arm. Two weeks later, in February, my mother slipped while climbing down the stairs and fractured her right leg. Seeing my mother's situation, my father fell sick because of low blood pressure. My grandfather was already ill recovering from three brain strokes. My three siblings were younger than I was, so my family depended on me.

My grandmother and mother had to be taken to the hospital simultaneously. My grandmother could not be operated on because of her age, and she came home with a plaster cast. My mother's leg was operated on and she stayed in the hospital for a week. That was the time when the COVID cases started peaking again and we had no help.

Until then, I had just worked outside the house. But I had not done much when it came to the home front. I had to focus all my energy on my family. I washed clothes, did dishes, and cleaned the house. I cooked food, looking up online recipes. I had never touched the iron before ironing my father's clothes every day. I burnt the bedsheet once and hit my hand on a running ceiling fan while folding the mosquito netting. I took care of my mother and grandmother, fed them, sponged them, helped change their clothes, and gave them medicines on time.

I helped my siblings with their homework. I managed both of our family's businesses—a fishery and a garment shop. The fishery had been run by my father who was still terribly unwell because of low blood pressure and rebuilding the business after the destructive cyclone was an uphill climb. In between I studied and did my school work. I had my Grade XI Final exams in this period too and came in first in class XI.

There wasn't a single word of appreciation for me, but for some force in heaven who everyone believed had pulled the family through the crisis. When I looked at my burnt fingers, injured feet and sweat-beaded brow, I felt a bit of resentment in my heart, and then I felt guilty for feeling this way.

I did find a way to vent my frustrations with self-harm. I would cut myself and try to focus on the physical pain to try and forget the emotional turmoil. But I injured myself too severely and couldn't help my brother with schoolwork. The next day, he was severely reprimanded in his online class. I realised this could be the way out this harming myself or anyone else, to the point where I would be rendered helpless. So I turned to music and writing instead. I told my journal what no one was ready to listen to, and music told me what no one else would. I truly felt comforted. I decided to help other people by giving them a safe space to share their feelings, and became a listener for "7 Cups of Tea," an online, anonymous mental health support initiative.

In all this time, I could not possibly ignore what was happening in the outside world. With more than three hundred thousand COVID cases per day, no number of helping hands could be too many for India. So I volunteered as a support person and helped hundreds of patients find hospital beds, oxygen cylinders, blood, food home delivery, and placed newly orphaned children, or children with parents hospitalised in temporary child care centres. In the daytime, I managed the household, my studies and took care of the family, and at night when everyone was asleep, I took night shifts to help the COVID victims.

Then in April, my grandmother was diagnosed with kidney failure and needed even more extensive care and a stricter diet. I handled everything in addition to the thirty-five organisations I worked with, and working as the student secretary of my school's student council. My days often began at 5:00a.m. and sometimes ended at 3:30a.m.

Throughout this period, I kept feeling like I would fall into depression. I felt stressed, yes, tense and extremely anxious too, but not for a single moment did I feel I wanted to do something drastic. Later I realised it was because I did not have the time or the mindset for it. I knew that I was bottling up a lot in my heart, and I needed to cry. Even if I found two minutes to myself, tears would not flow. I was emotionally dead working on autopilot. I knew if something happened to me, I would be taking down the entire family of ten members. So I persevered. I hardened my core.

Then my grandmother passed away towards the end of July 2021. That was the last straw. It was the push needed for everything inside to come pouring out. When the vehicle came to take her away, I would not let go of my grandma one bit. I became hysterical, screaming and shouting at the top of my lungs. My mother and sisters together could not pull me away. As soon the vehicle left, I fainted there on the street. I couldn't sleep all night, and when I did, my sleep was troubled with nightmares.

In our culture, the funeral for a person who passes away due to natural causes is held after eleven days. Because of the pandemic, only close relatives were present. The children and grandchildren are supposed to offer water to the deceased to calm their soul and send them off peacefully. As the priest held my hand and had me offer water, the promises I had made to my grandmother kept playing in my mind. She had only wished to go abroad with me and see me get married. I had also promised to give her a gold necklace when I started earning money. As I realised none of these promises could be honoured anymore, I felt like my heart was shattering. I almost wanted to turn back time and warn my younger self not to make promises she could not keep.

However, I have held on to her memory, and try to honour her wishes through every step I take.

In January 2022, I tested COVID positive. When I got the report, I wasn't scared. I told the virus in my body, "Good, after everything, we have come full circle and you have come to me. I will now show you what *strong* is."

In the beginning, I felt constantly weak and tired, and was down with a high fever. I couldn't keep down anything I ate, and could not smell or taste anything. I put on a mask at all times, even while sleeping, though I had a slight difficulty breathing. The residual cough accompanied me for many months.

Yet COVID could not stop me from doing a single thing I had planned out. I kept attending my classes, completing my projects, volunteering, working, and fighting with the virus. Neither did I let the virus disrupt a single moment of my routine, nor infect a single other member of my family—even though I was infected with the more transmittable variant of the virus. Five antibiotic tablets, and ten days later, I emerged from the ordeal stronger in a beautiful way. I felt more tired than usual, but when you're determined, nothing is impossible.

After I recovered I could feel I was different. I am an evolved individual, more mature, more resilient, not easily given to whims, or even bouts of anger with no reason. Miss as I might the old days, as change came upon me, I either had to accept the change, or risk being left behind, and the latter, I could not do. Once the heavy burden of worldly matters was put on my shoulders, I realised, I finally and truly grew up. I evolved.

∿

Author's Note: Covid 19 pandemic—just the mention of this phrase is enough to open a trove of memories, feelings and associations for all who were old enough to comprehend when the novel coronavirus struck the world. Most of us had to weather challenges in our own ways—social, physical and emotional. As a High School student in India living in a middle-class family of ten, so did I.

In India, the lockdown was imposed during the time of board exams-national level exams school students take in Grade 10 and 12, and that are believed to be the manifestation of one's performance during their entire school life. It is already a stressful affair, and for my class, which went into the lockdown after completing Grade 10 Boards and came out of the lockdown only to take Grade 12 Boards, the pressure was tremendous. One of my friends succumbed to this pressure and took her own life, an experience that shook me to the core. Even though she was lively and always surrounded by many, we came to know she actually felt very lonely and left out.

These experiences made me realise the importance of mental health and that our experiences do matter. The result was "The Evolution," a reminiscence of my journey during Covid. It encompasses the sweet and the bitter, the rays of hope and the phases of darkness and the emotions, expectations and contrasting thoughts. I share it with the global community with the hope that, maybe someday, it will give someone the last strand of hope they are looking for to hold on, and tell them, that indeed, they are not alone.

YOUTHLINE

YouthLine is a free teen-to-teen crisis support and helpline.

You can call 877-968-8491, Text 839863 or online.

On Fire

By Roodley Merilo

The world is *literally* on fire,
This isn't a metaphor
Although it could have been
Australia's forest fires were burning just as bright
As the hatred we had towards one another
Sparked by the death of George Floyd
Ignited cop cars became the latest of many tragedies, But I
    am stuck in my bed

[pause]

Unable to get up but still yearning
Caught in this in-between
Wanting to better myself
But being held back by
A doubt-filled mind
Force feeding me thoughts of this cruel reality
Noting the fact that I'm alone in this room,
No one has checked up on me in months
I should be failing three different classes
My youth has been robbed from me
Because I'm unable to get up
To get out of this bed

Trapped by these four walls,
My desolate room
Surrounded by dirty clothing land mines
Mom circles back to drop *the mind-blowing revelation* that,
     my room is a mess

[pause]

But doesn't seem to notice
that I am a mess

[pause]

My life is a mess

[pause]

The whole world is a mess
So why do you draw the line at my room?

[pause]

I know mental health is a joke in this household
But I can no longer go on laughing
The hopeful boy you once knew is now just a memory
I wish I could go back,
Back to the simpler times, the carefree times
Where my world was exclusive to the toys in my room
Back where I shared a laugh with my friends
Where I could have hugged them a little tighter
Held them a little closer
Before they decided to treat their wrist like a weekly
     haircut appointment just one of many, warping their
     bodies into something

Less than admirable
No longer the friend which I once admired
But the mirror reflection I fear

[pause]

Why can't I get up
Why am I lying here
It's starting to get uncomfortable
My back is hurting
I need to pee
I haven't eaten in weeks
No!
Cereal is not a dinner
And chips are not a meal
But I can't seem to summon the courage to get up,
Get up
Get up
Come on you can do it

[pause]

Five steps never seemed so far before
What's the point anyways
I'm just gonna waste away my days on Zoom
Not learning a thing
But still getting A's
By pressing unmute
Just to say Roodley Merilo is present
But not fully here

[pause]

But lying here doesn't seem like the solution
I don't know if happiness is another fairytale lie
But it's something I want to strive for
Don't wanna end up like my brothers,
Or another failed child the way my father would put it
Need to get all "A's"
'Cause that's the only time he seemed proud of me
Feeling like I have to be greater than Michelangelo or
    Shakespeare
Needing to reinvent the wheel
And discover a new element to name it "Rood-anium"
So that maybe I can feel like I'm worth something
But all that only starts if I get up
So you need to
GET THE F__ UP!

[don't pause]

GET
UP
Roodley!

∾

Author's Note: I created this piece to really highlight
the mental battle many young teens face on a day to day.
    Mostly I wanted to portray the negative feelings many of
us felt during the pandemic; and how the pandemic itself
made everything harder with online learning and the
dreadful place the world was in. I hope when people read
this they take away how simply getting up, despite all the
adversity, can be the most powerful thing you can do.

THE MENTAL HEALTH COALITION

The MHC is dedicated to addressing the mental health needs of the community.

Reach out by texting COALITION to 741741.

Pandemic 2021

By Deandre Avant

It's amazing to believe what was going to be the best year ever turned into the beginning of what was thought to be the end. 2019 was my original year to graduate high school. Only because of a near ending romance my chance at passing a class on time was fatal. Not only did I lose the girl of my dreams, I lost respect from my mother and I ultimately repeated senior year.

Coming back into the school I've already been in for four years, expecting new changes and a better me, I ended up having the most derailed year of school. Only a month after my birthday I had to stop going to in-person school because of a new pandemic.

I predicted coronavirus would last only two weeks, which turned into the rest of the school year and my losing my job to then not having money to having good and bad days for when I can vs cannot eat. Praying for a miracle as I started 2020 living in a shelter program that currently I'm still in called Bridge Over Troubled Waters; having to quarantine in the building because other people around me are getting this new disease; then to move to Brighton in August 2020 into my own room but not be able to celebrate New Year's with my family because someone in this new building caught the disease.

I've been at Bunker Hill for a year but I'm leaving because I need to make more money to survive vs being educated in the career path I'm choosing. I'm feeling the pressure throughout this whole time to not self-harm, to not smoke, to not drink, to not jump off a building or anything negative. I'm having to relearn what love is while being in the position where it seems as if there is no love for me to feel.

BLM as a movement progresses because of white cops wanting to murder more people.

Living in Downtown Boston from January to July, I had to walk past military weapons controlled by privileged white men assigned to murder anyone in the vision of Trump. I watched people from the third floor of the building run away in fear from police all over Massachusetts in parts no one has even heard from. The next morning the store windows were broken into, graffiti everywhere, people in shock over the destruction that was supposed to be a peaceful movement.

Then I had to get tested the following morning because of my concern I still might get the virus.

It was the latter half of 2020 when things finally started to get better for my life. This pandemic has given me a lot of time to reflect on past wrongs from high school and everything within the years I was in high school thinking of better ways to live the dreams I never lost sight of but had to pursue a little later than I had planned.

I'm Jamaican, Chinese from my mother's side and mostly African American on my father's side. I'm a hybrid, and both of my cultures suffered all of 2020. I can only imagine what my two families would say to everything that happened and what was worse for which side.

What would be worse is the fact that even when Biden got elected he made the choice of who's better by signing a bill within a year versus a bill that's been needed for centuries.

Having responsibilities isn't usually a problem but it is when the virus isn't over yet. The only person in the medical profession I know who is aware the virus isn't over is my mother. She knows the vaccines aren't the final answer because this is still very new. As per usual in my life her predictions are correct because now there's a new vaccine variant we can take for us to have a chance at being safe. Doesn't guarantee the vaccine could protect us especially since I had to change work plans because two co-workers who were both vaccinated got the virus. My building manager was trying to force the vaccine on us but any risk of taking it for me could be fatal.

Looking back on my feelings, for me it's all about what choices you decide and if taking the vaccine is good or bad for you. For me it doesn't make sense because I barely get sick, plus I'm always active, and there's more to COVID including this new variant Omicron. It's been a struggle to make so many choices and decisions and being surrounded by people even when wanting to be by myself. It's also a question of what it would be like if the pandemic didn't exist.

Would these many decisions have to be made in the normal life that everyone was used to? Or would everything be discarded because it's a new day where everyone is attempting to feel good?

Everyone is trying to do their part to the fullest of abilities in this day and age to be concerned with mental health. Mental health was never a concern in my lifetime up until we reached the new decade. It's amazing how much hope one single person can have for a world that is so cruel and continues to be reconstructed from past norms. Never will I be able to understand how life got us to the point where we are right now. I know what I want as of now but it's a question of when will this pandemic be over for real? Will masks still be relevant in the next five years while I'm still trying to become the successful architect I've been working hard to become?

Asking so many of these questions and not knowing if the answers will be right for the moment. Everyone sees a 6' 2" male dancing down the street thinking he's the happiest lucky guy on the planet. When in all reality I'm dancing the pain away from the negative energy this pandemic has put onto myself. Hoping that one day the world can return to a safe normal where people's rights are respected. Equality can be a must instead of an option, where millennials aren't telling the people who come after them what's possible versus what's not; creating families with positive morals rather than broken up family mentalities.

This pandemic is a bar graph in my life and will continue for who knows how long. Next year's hopes for me are that we can continue improving our human society, but also being safe physically and mentally. My 2019 was bad, 2020 was worse, and 2021 was better than the previous but there was room for improvement. 2022 for me will hopefully be better and be a great year.

~

Author's Note: I'm Deandre Avant and this story is basically my life for the last two to three years. The pandemic has its highs and lows in terms of me. Just like everybody else I've struggled in many ways, changed my views on life, helped out people even when I could barely help myself. I hope every reader knows and understands that life isn't perfect even when you have high hopes and do the right thing. Emotions are gonna be prevalent but different depending on who you are.

Not only do I want to thank Dmae and everyone from MediaRites for this amazing opportunity, but I'd love to also thank the most important person in my life. My girlfriend Kailyn Dubuisson who has been a strong support system for me during the pandemic. She got me to believe that anything is possible no matter how hard life can be for someone. When I wasn't talking to my family, she was the one and only person I could depend on. Even when things were rough for her, Kai would never leave me hanging and that's what I love the most about her. She's the sweetest person in my life and a fantastic partner to be with in a relationship.

DON'T CALL THE POLICE

This is an online database and directory of community-based resources as an alternative to call the police or 911.

https://dontcallthepolice.com

A Quarantine Poem
(or The Best Ways to Dull the Ache in My Boredom)

By Niko Boskovic

It's been a week of home-cooked meals and sleeping in too
    late
A steady thrum of washing the dust out of curtains
organizing drawers to better serve our needs when
we will pour back out into these streets
unafraid of each other
feeling full of glad tidings
for the sheer human connection
after months of isolation.

But that's something to look forward to
as we have weeks to go
books to read
wine to drink
people to dream about
fantasies to morph into new realities someday
after this is over.
People will die.

How heavily this weighs on our collective conscience
is the reason it's so easy to
leave the front door locked for hours untouched

put the kettle on for the umpteenth time

work to organize our lives in some way

so this will never happen again

until of course it does.

Let us apologize to everyone who agonizes

lungs filling with fluid

respirators made secondhand

hospital staff not seeing a person but a statistic —

playing God

not with pulled wings from butterflies

legs torn from the orb of a daddy long leg

ants decimated by the scope of the magnifying glass

but in the perfect storm created by us.

Forgive us this global trespass

unto our fellow human who understands

the value in our connectedness

even as it kills us.

~

Author's Note: This is one of three poems I wrote in the last two years while taking an advanced poetry writing class. The other two are also included in this book. Like all my poems, they are very personal (as all poetry is), and are informed by my lived experience as a minimally-speaking autistic who uses a letterboard to communicate.

I make poetry in my head all the time out of the things I see around me. For example, I have been thinking about the way this year has differed from past years when I wasn't

able to communicate and the way I felt as a receiver—
never a giver—of presents; how it feels to be someone's
hoped-for face when they open the door; what the smell of
snow in Portland tasted like. I want to write about it all. In
any case, the poems still inside me will keep coming out for
as long as someone is willing to hold the letterboard up to
my gaze.

YOUTH ERA

Youth Era creates solutions for communities that look beyond short-term assistance and toward sustainable support for the many.

More Than a Joke

By Isabella Santana

"I'm going to kill myself," I said as I laughed with my friend about the "D" I received on my algebra test. Back then, I used to see suicide as a joke. My friends and I would send each other knife emojis and skulls back then. I would giggle about ending my life because of a bad grade in a science class or a fight with my parents. Naive and immature, I could not grasp the severity of suicide. I did not really understand what it meant to want to kill yourself. I did not see how much people who wanted to kill themselves suffered. I saw it as something wrong, yet something so rare it was laughable.

Flash forward a year to the first time a legitimately suicidal thought crossed my head. A fallout with my friends led to an extreme depression that lasted the entirety of my freshman year of high school. During spring, however, everything got significantly worse. I did not just feel lonely, I felt completely isolated from the rest of the world. I felt tortured, so desperate for conversation I spent my lunchtimes counting the number of words people spoke to me. After a while of this agony, I began to wonder if I was the problem. I convinced myself I created my own place in hell. At night, I would cry thinking about how nobody loved me or cared about me.

Eventually, I began to lean towards death. It seemed like a simple way out of all my problems.

It appealed to me. I had the means at home: pills, sharp objects, bedsheets. I told myself this: if life ever got so painful I could no longer see a will to live, I would take every single pill in the medicine cabinet and die. I never tried it. I held onto the hope things would get better, and they did . . . after I was forced into therapy. For a solid eight months, my mental health remained stable. I didn't think about suicide. I still joked about it, lying to myself and saying it was my way of coping. Life felt decent for some time. I thought the odds would turn in my favor and things would go back to how they were.

I couldn't have been more wrong.

The following years were the most challenging months of my life. It began on March 13, 2020, when the world went into a total shutdown. My spiral downwards started with a physical decline. A simple diet that began after New Year's Day turned into anorexia nervosa. In June, my family loaded itself into our car and drove all the way to Wickenburg, Arizona. I spent two and a half months at an eating disorder facility, where I faked recovery and happiness. I came home in a good physical condition, but eager to relapse.

I wanted to relapse, and that's exactly what I did. I took no time in sneaking in old behaviors and introducing new ones. As I did, my mental state worsened. My depression's severity shot up exponentially. With it came the reintroduction of suicidal thoughts, which only seemed to worsen as my dosage of Prozac increased. At some point, I stopped taking my antidepressants; a big mistake, because doing so can cause extreme drops in serotonin. I ended up becoming the most depressed I'd ever been.

Life was painful—every day the same cycle of restriction and shame. I resorted to drugs to numb the pain of starvation, but not even that could ease the pain I felt inside. I lost sense of my family values: I stopped listening to my parents and their advice, I pushed my sisters away, and I did not want anybody else's concern or help. This hopelessness and despair led me to my final resort: suicide.

I remember my first attempt in November quite vividly. I found hydrocodone in my mom's medicine cabinet; painkillers prescribed to her after a back injury. I sneaked twelve pills into my room. One night, I took ten, saving two for the next time I wanted to get high. I really had no idea what they would do to me; all I knew was I wanted my pain to end. I handed myself over to death that day, hoping that it would take me away from this world.

It didn't happen. I woke up the next morning extremely hungover, but alive.

Here's the thing about suicide. It's a parasite that consumes its host. It becomes the only thing in the host's mind. I used every single waking second following my first attempt planning my next attempt. This time, I would starve myself to death. This time, I would succeed.

I almost did. I remember the heart palpitations, the terrifying EKG results, the dizziness, and lightheadedness. I remember how much it hurt to get up every day, watching those around me eat while I ate nothing. I remember being transferred to another eating disorder facility, where I immediately got a feeding tube. Getting that close to death terrified me, but in a sick way, it also excited me.

Once again, I restored the weight I lost and restored my old, happy self. Unfortunately, those feelings of happiness went away quickly. Once again, I found myself planning my death.

In the next five months, I would try to kill myself over five times. Those five months blurred past me; I can't recall much from that time. I do, however, remember how much I suffered.

I went through days where suicide was literally the only thing I could think about. I saw a glass bottle and thought about how I would kill myself with it. I looked at my bedsheets and wondered if I could hang or strangle myself with them. When driving, I tried to work up the courage to jump out of the car and onto the freeway.

People walked on eggshells around me, worried that if they said the wrong thing I would attempt suicide. My relationships with my family fractured, as I became more violent and aggressive. My self-destructive behaviors completely spiraled out of control. I made multiple trips to psychiatric hospitals, riding in ambulances and even a cop car to make sure I would get there safely.

At one point, I felt so exhausted. Not exhausted of living, exhausted of feeling suicidal. It took up all my mental and physical energy. I spent so many nights curled up in a ball in my bed, begging for the thoughts to stop, but they wouldn't go away. I would try so hard to focus on something else, but a little frustration or inconvenience upset me so much, suicide felt like the only answer to my problem. My life felt like it was falling apart, the little things that gave me stability falling into a chasm of emptiness. My fight against my demons got closer to its end, and I wasn't the victor.

The weight of existence, the pain of living when feeling suicidal crushed me slowly. I tight-roped between life and death, dangerously teetering towards death. I tried so hard to keep myself afloat but all I did was sink deeper into my thoughts and feelings. I couldn't enjoy anything, I saw no meaning in life, I convinced myself my life would be painful forever.

Everything felt hopeless, I felt helpless. My thoughts sucked me under and took all joy out of my life. I needed someone to save me, but only I could save myself. Nobody could save me from me. I couldn't stop my behaviors. It seemed as if my fate to die by suicide was sealed.

And yet, I survived.

By some miracle, I made it to the other side. I found happiness and meaning in life again. I dedicated myself to my recovery and worked hard every single day to stay mentally stable.

It took all my energy and effort, and it couldn't have been more worth it.

My views of life completely changed as I went through my recovery. Most changed was my view on suicide. In the past, I considered it a joke, later as a last resort, then as something comforting.

Now, I see suicide for what it really is: a lie. The promise of an escape, an easy way out of misery. Yet, the only way to do it is to put oneself through more pain and fear. Suicide tells its victims that others will be happy without them. This couldn't be farther from the truth. My loved ones suffered so deeply while I remained in an unstable condition. Suicide construes the meaning of every little word that comes out of someone's mouth. It feeds into its victims' deepest fear and uses it against them.

Now that I see suicide's true nature, I can fight against it. I can also bring awareness and help people through my story. The world needs to change its view on suicide, starting off with the way it is used in conversation. Phrases like "I want to die" or "I'm going to kill myself" should never be thrown into everyday conversation as if it's nothing. Suicide is real and terrifying. It never was and never will be okay to treat it like a joke. Throwing suicide into everyday conversation further reinforces the idea that suicide is not a big enough problem for it to require a serious conversation surrounding it. Suicide is a huge problem; it's killing people of all ages. Kids and young adults are experiencing the brunt of it. Why does a large chunk of society think suicide is nothing more than a little joke?

I strongly believe the culprit is ignorance. People simply don't know what it's like to be suicidal.

They don't understand suicidal thoughts never go away. I learned how to live with them and decrease their frequency of them, but they're always sitting there in the corner of my mind, waiting for the right time to hack into my brain and take over.

I refuse to joke about suicide now because I know firsthand how painful it is to be suicidal. Still, I experience moments where my mind is consumed by suicidal thoughts. Every time that happens, however, I try my hardest to not give in. I also make an enormous effort to not play it off like a joke.

The bottom line is this: suicide is not okay. It's not the answer, it's not a saving grace. It ruins lives and consumes people completely. Like bacteria, it multiplies uncontrollably.

Sometimes, it feels as if there is no way to stop it. However, I know from experience it is possible to stop it. It's possible to live a better life and begin seeing suicide for what it truly is.

As painful as it is to let go of something that once was comforting, it's even more painful to hold on and remain miserable. As basic as it sounds, I know in my heart that recovery is possible, and so so worth it.

My whole life, I've been told that I have a bright future ahead of me. I used to be unable to see it.

I used to toss my life around, not caring what happened to me. Suicide used to be my comforter, even though it destroyed me. I will fight to raise awareness about suicide and change the way it is used in conversation. Life will get hard again, I know that. This time, however, instead of staying stuck in my hell, I will rise. I will learn to love life again, and, I will live.

～

Author's Note: I wrote this piece in light of my experience with suicide and my observations of how my generation talks about suicide. I noticed that my generation likes to throw around suicide in conversation as if the word itself is nothing but part of a game of hot potato. I want people of all ages, but especially people of my generation, to think before saying something like: "I'm going to kill myself" or "I want to die."

My piece is tear-stained pillows and scratchy throats. It's real. I hope my audience can feel the vulnerability through the words. My goal in this piece is not to shame but to usher new ideas and perspectives into the minds of those who read my piece. Suicide truly is no joke. I firmly believe that the world needs to hear this.

NATIONAL SUICIDE PREVENTION LIFELINE.

The Lifeline is a 24 hour toll-free phone line for people in suicidal crisis.

1-800-273-TALK
or Dial/Text 988

Smile

By Ellenore "Ella" Celko

BZZT!
Bestie
DING!
Hey...
I Dont
want to
Be friends
anymore
ur really
annoying
So dont
talk to
me any-
more...
teacher:
are you
there?
ZOOM CHAT
She is ProBaBly crying cause She has no friends
I DID it!
LMAO
BZZT!
BZZT!
SLAM

IM JUS+ BEING MYSELF WHAt DID I DO WRONG? WHY DOES EVERYONE HATE ME? WHY?! WHY AM I SO UGLY WHY AM I SUCH A FREAK?!
WHY ME?!
gets up
thunk
CRASH
hon? what happened?! im coming in!
NO!!! WAIT
What happened to the plant?
turn around why aren't you in class?
hon?

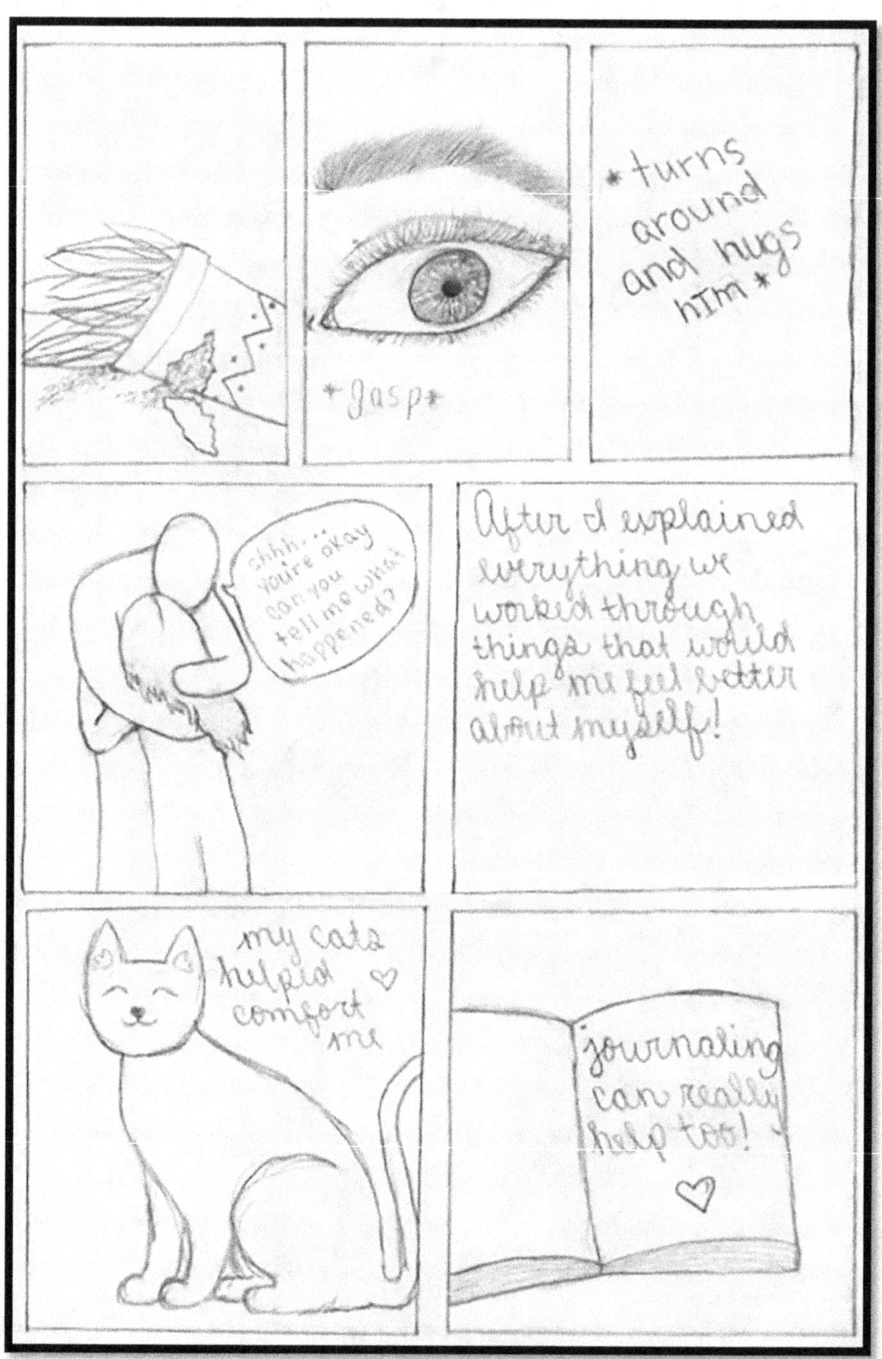
gasp
* turns around and hugs hIm *
shhh... you're okay can you tell me what happened?
After I explained everything we worked through things that would help me feel better about myself!
my cats helped comfort me
journaling can really help too!

and I'm in a much better place now!
I have good friends!
And It Will All Be Okay!
if you're going through stuff...
just know...
IT WILL GET BETTER
you're not alone.
don't give up. stay strong.
people DO care.

THE JED FOUNDATION

The Jed Foundation empowers teens and young adults with the skills and support to grow into healthy, thriving adults.

Part II

. . . That Happened

The Many Who Don't Fit In

By Jenell Theobald

"Please wait. The meeting host will let you in soon."

I am sitting in the study room by myself, staring at the words on the screen. It is a golden autumn afternoon in 2021. The second year of the pandemic, of social isolation, of being stuck at home. The tick tock of the clock is the only sound at the moment. The computer tells me it's a little past starting time. Finally, I am let in, and another session of my social skills training classes is on.

Something is a bit off, though. My coaches don't seem as energetic and enthusiastic today. And, there are fewer people than usual. One person is missing. Because this is quite an expensive self-paid small group class, no one ever misses class, so today's smaller class size is noticeable. But it's probably nothing. He probably just went on vacation. But he didn't show up to the next class either, or the class after that. Then I found out he died by suicide. My heart twisted, and a wave of sorrow washed over me.

In this class, we are a group of "different" youth, outsiders. We have always been teased or ignored. We lack social and communication skills. We don't have many friends, if any at all.

Most of us have been diagnosed with autism. We don't fit into the social setting around us. And like most autistic kids, we experience different degrees of depression. We all have had similar experiences of struggling to fit in, so we understand each other. The missing student was my homework partner a few weeks back. Halfway through our conversation, he broke down, yelling that his life was meaningless. His parents apologized to me, and our conversation had to end early. The thought still gnaws at my conscience: would things have turned out differently if I'd said something earlier. The thought still gnaws at my conscience: would things have turned out differently if I'd said something?

Our nation is facing a severe mental health crisis right now. Before the pandemic started, Oregon, where I live, had one fourth of its population living with disabilities, most of them mental. The pandemic made things even worse. Stories like this happen all the time. Everyone knows somebody who needs help: a friend, relative, neighbor, classmate . . . Mental healthcare is so overbooked. All of the reputable professionals have very long waiting lists. Finding a specialist is hard, much less an in-network one. I am one of the lucky ones who eventually climbed out of the abyss. But many are not as lucky.

Sadly, it has been this way throughout most of human history, some people get left behind for reasons outside of their control. Nowadays, thanks to many dedicated people who worked tirelessly for the equality they believe in, we live in a society where everyone has equal rights, no matter their background or condition – at least in theory. To help ensure this is more than just an empty slogan, I recently have joined the cause to fight for some historically marginalized communities.

One of my projects was advocacy for the building of a cultural heritage garden at Block 14 of Lone Fir Cemetery. Block 14 is an important piece of local history that has been forgotten, intentionally or unintentionally. Two groups of people are sheltered beneath.

The first group is over two hundred of Dr. Hawthorne's asylum patients. The Oregon Hospital for the Insane was the first hospital for mental illness in Oregon. Known for his humanity, Dr. Hawthorne paid out of his own pocket for hundreds of burials, not only those with mental illness, but also those whose families were absent, or were living in poverty, physically disabled, or displayed behavior not accepted by society. Sometimes I wonder how many in my training class would be buried there if we had lived back then.

The second group is Chinese workers who built much of the infrastructure in our area, often underpaid and in dangerous working conditions, resulting in many deaths. They were buried in Block 14 temporarily until their bodies could be shipped back to their home villages in China. Yet for many, especially women and children, Block 14 became their permanent resting place. Over time, the gravestones were destroyed and their stories were forgotten, as if their existence had no importance to the people who used the infrastructure these Chinese gave their lives to build.

The city intended to sell the land of Block 14 for development, but multiple groups raised concerns, especially after human remains were discovered in 2005. Although plans were drawn up for a cultural heritage garden that would honor both groups in the 1990s, there was never any funding. Then, in 2019, Oregon Metro passed a parks and nature bond that would prioritize projects that promoted diversity. However, for a long time, the garden was not part of the discussion list. So the Lone Fir Cemetery Foundation reached out. I was the first one to answer the call. I wrote a sample letter to Metro and sent it to some social groups I'm in.

Because of this, twenty-five other students also wrote their own letters. The letter campaign eventually led to $4 million being allocated to the project, making the Foundation's two-decades-long dream a reality. Two groups of marginalized people resting at Block 14 finally would be recognized.

Although our country has become more and more inclusive, we all understand there is no such thing as an ideal world. For around ten years, the city I live in hasn't had any committee to serve people with disabilities. So another project I accomplished lately is successfully convincing my city to reinstate the ADA advisory committee. I am now serving on this board.

Racism, xenophobia, and all the other -isms and phobias will always be problems, at least for the foreseeable future. There will always be people who struggle with mental health.

There will always be those groups of people that have it worse than everyone else. But the world is getting better every day, thanks to the people who keep bending the arc of the moral universe toward justice. Nowadays, people are generally understanding and accepting of those with physical disabilities, yet many don't realize that mental disabilities are disabilities, too. I know I will do my part to help spread awareness of this, and continue to fight for those that are marginalized or left behind. Perhaps there is nothing I can do for my classmate, but I can help prevent future cases, so nothing like this happens again.

∽

Author's Note: I was born with physical and mental disabilities, including autism, so I've always struggled to fit in. I was bullied and excluded, and switched schools a lot, having attended seven by the time I was in fifth grade. It wasn't until then that I made my first close friend. I've also had bouts of depression. Still, I'm one of the lucky ones, relatively speaking. I got a lot of help from many different therapists and counselors. Some of my fondest memories are from when I was at Camp Meadowood Springs, a summer camp for kids with social and communication difficulties. The camp was sponsored by the Oregon Elks, and they are the ones who got me to think seriously about community service.

But there are many who are unable to get the help they need, and continue to suffer alone, especially during this pandemic. Some people even take their own lives to escape their pain. This is such a critical issue for the country, yet it gets far less attention than it should. I know what it's like to struggle with mental illness. I hope that my readers will come away knowing a little bit what it's like as well. I want to speak up for those who can't speak for themselves and bring greater awareness to these important issues. If I don't, who will?

AUTISM SOCIETY

Autism Society is an organization working to increase public awareness about day-to-day issues about people across the spectrum.

home • sick • ness
● *longing for a place you aren't sure exists* ●

By Cara Chen

"i'm home," i say to myself,
in this box of a room with its lilac walls
the exact shade i'd picked out when i was six.

"i'm home,"
amid the tangle of cobwebs clinging to the fan,
stubbornly, with a strength
foreign to me. or maybe not—
because sometimes i hurt so much
i think i must be both the strongest and the weakest person
    in the world.

"i'm home,"
in a library that smells like old chips and mildewed carpets
    amber-crystalled light slanting in from the windows
and a skylight never cracked open.
those shelves, endless to a child
seem to shuffle closer as i grow;
or maybe it's just my
hopeless imagination.

"i'm home,"
i say, to a house too empty for my soul. a house that, if given
    the chance,
would swallow me up—teeth and hair and all
until there was nothing of me left for myself.

"maybe this is home," i say
my words echoing, tinted lilac and suffused with spider-
    silk.
maybe this is home, this place where
if you aren't careful,
could become so much of *you* that you forget how to be
    anything else.

reasons why wanderlust exists

~

Author's Note: Although not pandemic-centered, I believe that loneliness has become a significant part of the aftershocks of the pandemic and should be addressed. This is my best attempt to put my experiences into writing. "home • sick • ness," is about longing for something old and warm and familiar and finding that it doesn't suit you anymore, that you've outgrown it and now you have to either shed it like an old skin or let it define who you are. It's a boxed-in sort of loneliness, where something you used to like or do separates you from the rest of the world and you have to either let it go or let the rest of the world fly by past your fingertips.

I think, for many of us, loneliness feels interminable, something so stubborn and enduring that we're not sure we'll ever be able to get rid of it, even when the world opens back up; it's something I struggle with daily. But I think that we can work together to overcome loneliness by talking about it and interacting with each other. Maybe we can even bond over shared loneliness.

I hope, then, that my written words can convey this feeling better than my spoken words have ever been able to; I hope that my poems can be a tool for understanding and overcoming loneliness.

Thank you for reading.

THE TREVOR PROJECT

The Trevor Project offers accredited life-saving and life-affirming programs and services the LGBTQ youth to create safe, accepting, and inclusive environments online or over the phone.

During and Now

By Journeya

God, I'm not even sure where to begin. In my head, my junior year remains murky. It is like I'm standing in the middle of a contemporary memory but I have no sense of direction. I get vertigo trying to recall the happenings in that year and when it is mentioned I literally feel an electrical shock to my frontal cortex; the effect of the collected trauma from that year.

The year 2020 all happened in just a few rooms in my house and one small computer screen. The school year was short lived, like two blinks. I remember how much my butt and legs hurt from sitting in my 1980's wicker desk chair for eight plus hours, but that was the worst of it.

Online school was all right for me academically, and sometimes I feel a sort of survivor's guilt *because* it was all right. Being at home in solitude was like breathing new found air that was mine, all mine. The lockdown of the school was earth shattering in all the right ways. So many of my peers fell to the solitude while I was riding on it like I was Jack and it was the growing beanstalk. I have the solitude to thank for who I am now.

I remember we began school much later than in person, around 9:00am. We had a two-hour break to catch up on work and for lunch. I used it for mostly my hobbies such as yoga, meditation, and hikes when it was warm out. During the winter months I used the two hours to nap. The winter months were extremely hard to tolerate because there was nowhere to go. Our school fluctuated between completely online and hybrid learning. When we were in school they gave us Wednesdays off to deep clean the school.

When we started the school year the teachers were too ambitious and the workload ended up being overwhelming for me and my peers. Towards the middle of the year they started to catch on that kids were severely ill, mentally and physically, from the amount of school work under the pandemic circumstances. It was a hard break for everyone as well as a much-needed reality check on the impact mental health has. We worked around the clock so much I can remember eating at the computer with my leg bouncing rapidly as my school time spread into my dinner time. We ended the school day around 2:00pm but as we were working from home with this massive workload it never seemed to *actually* end. In this year I took IB Art so I would spend a lot of time after hours, including the whole two hours of break a couple times, working on those projects. My bedroom was my art space, work space, and safe space. It never really was a good safe space though because of crashing dualities.

After

In April, still in my junior year, I saw the beige brick walls of my school halls for one full day. It had been almost a year of hybrid learning and now they gave us the option to go in full time or stay online for the rest of the year. I was one who chose to go back. I felt it was time.

There had been times in the year when I would go in to pick up school supplies and it was always an odd experience that caused anxiety. A lot of trauma from the fear of people and memories of leaving the school so abruptly would come up.

My feelings about the first day, however, weren't anything like that. I was very excited, maybe even joyful. Walking into the school I wore an outfit that I had put together myself so that wearing it made me feel like I was an accomplished model. I was comfortable in my own skin.

I felt unstoppable and ready to mingle and laugh with the outside world again. But the day did not turn out as it had gone in my head, which was running with anticipation.

The halls were barren. Quite barren. Out of the hundreds of students, only a few were in school. Most were online. Even during the lunch rush hour there was a stark difference in the number of people from previous years. I remember being comforted by the lack of people, but also disappointed and crushed by it. There were only one to four kids in each of my classes including myself. Now, we are talking about a school with an average total of 1,036 kids. To paint a picture: a mix of all the economic classes and majority BIPOC. The normal class sizes are usually twenty to thirty.

No one wanted to talk; the environment was already filled with silence and with teachers awkwardly trying to make things lighter when they too had clearly shut down or given up. In all honesty I remember being able to hear my own heartbeat and wanting to tear out of my skin to escape the roaring stillness. The two kids who *did* talk had nothing nice to say. Earlier in the year I had shaved my head for expressionistic purposes. These kids chose to point it out quite loudly.

They made hurtful comments on my baldness and how I dressed. I realized in the moment I had become a physical embodiment of my true self, and I was a target. Getting introduced back into the mean kindergarten words of public school was going to be my ball and chain this year.

Throughout the year I experienced more bullying on my physical appearance. Someone took a picture of my bald head and posted on Snapchat saying some ignorant comment I don't care to repeat, and another group regressed back into pre-k years commenting on how big my ankles looked. Never have I had to deal with this much bullying on physical appearance before. Clearly, we were all in a lot of pain one way or another and were dealing with it in our own pitiful ways.

The day grew heavy very fast and I was beginning to notice the intense pain in my back from the four binders and a Chromebook in my backpack. I hadn't experienced that in quite some time, and I had *not* missed it. I had not gone outside in many hours and felt the weight of that too. Since online learning I wasn't used to not having fresh air when I wanted. And that was crazy. *That* was *crazy*. To be confined for eight hours or more with no ability to seek our own life-giving resources. To not be able to sit in the grass and look at the sky. To be quelled from dance and play, and to have your childhood energy get a smack on the wrist like in the good ol' days. Maybe *I'm* crazy, but this lifestyle isn't right and it never was.

I left that building of grey and beige walls sulking and feeling like an embodiment of the colors themselves. There were another two months to go, and I was hopeful for the future but I left feeling most of my life force taken from me.

Now

Now it is July 2022. I am far away from high school and that building. That *place*. A place I have a long line of memories to heal from now that I'm a graduate.

I was not able to keep the same high spirit I had in April through my time at school in the months and year that followed. Nor was I able to protect a lot of my steady confidence I had cultivated in my solitude. The public school system was, and continues to be a rude, harsh, and vile awakening. Coming back after the lockdowns, I became very aware that through the previous ten years of public school, I ran on adrenaline and survival instincts. The mean words from kids commenting on my skin, my hair, and my weight. The social pack mentality where the big groups pick on, bully and spread hate. The undying fear for your

entire future if you miss *one* assignment. The enforced
control of one's bodily functions when denied food,
bathroom, or water. Wearing pants and baggy tees on hot
scalding days because if you wear shorts or a tank you'll be
told to change. Stuffing your face with food 'cause you only
get twenty minutes for lunch. The security guards
bellowing at students who try to sneak some food to their
class 'cause they didn't finish eating. The loud crowds and
glaring lights; no shadow of any object in sight.

Security guards following you into the bathroom to see
that you don't "misbehave." Gun and bomb threat
notification emails that come in the night. School shootings.
Need I go on? The education system breaks you down and
buries you. Starting at 7:00 AM on the weekdays.

"Don't move. Be still." An echo and mirror of my mind
during the school days.

I become more and more shocked at how parents have
been able to send their children into these *places* for so
long.

Going back in person for my senior year was
tremendously hard on my mental health, so I was able to
work something out with my school that allowed me to go
into school every other day. My spirit and body seemingly
had taken a stand to things going back to "normal" for me
and I was okay with that. Coming back from distance
learning, played "Ring Around the Rosie" with my state of
mind. I was walking on split ground. On one side I walked
in a feeling of new, mature, ready to take on the world
graduate. That left. Only to get confiscated back. And then
on the other side, a sophomore; small and still. Frozen in a
pre-lockdown reality. Instead of feeling like school was my
focused purpose as in past years, I was just there. Doing my
time. I was ready to be out. I couldn't stand the boxy halls
anymore. I had gotten a taste of something other than the
public-school standard and I wanted to get out sooner
rather than later. Different from how my peers felt. I floated

through the school halls like a ghost in my senior year. I stood between the split, phasing in and out until I was able to truly break free. My mind, energy, and interests had left high school. I just had to physically walk across the stage.

Seeing, as well as being around, people almost daily came with its blessings and growing pains. I made many new friends I hadn't been close with in the years before the pandemic. It was rejuvenating to surround myself with people and a new tribe. I had to move past the heavy fear of being around others again, especially after my school lifted the masks, and I had to relearn how to let go and experience joy.

Though I was distanced from it because I was a senior, I heard a lot about how socially stunted the underclassmen seemed to be. I've heard reports of horrific stories of how students acted towards teachers and each other. To give a few examples, a group of students harassed people by barking at them. There were physical fights about three times a month, which is abnormal, and intense bullying. All of this was mostly directed at the LGBTQ+ community. For a period of time we had a situation in a history class where a couple of kids drew a Nazi symbol and other obscene things on a worksheet and handed it in to their teacher. The teacher was Jewish, and to my understanding the students knew that beforehand. I've noticed some teachers are contemplating taking a new career path. Whether it's because of these past two years catching up with them or the social state of the underclassmen, I don't know.

The Before, After, and Now moments create a bilious mix. These past few years have been *odd* to say the very least. Pulling us left and right. Backwards and forwards. Upside down and back again. Up until this very moment, writing this now, I don't think I took graduating from high school seriously. I don't think I *really* comprehended the absolute theme park roller coaster ride I endured. And here I am on the other side. The day after graduation the clothes

on my back felt different; my tunnel vision had cleared up.
It all came full circle and everything was right again.
Though this pandemic hit me in a lot of different ways, I am
grateful for the lockdowns that led me to realize what I
could really make of myself.

~

Author's Note: If there's anything I want readers to
gain from this piece and story, it's seeing the importance of
community, raw communication, and using your voice. I
also wanted to acknowledge the chaos going on within us
all instead of pushing along and seeking to find the
"normal." Going through this piece and typing these words
on to the screen was therapy for me. It processed what was
going on around me in real time. I hope this piece may help
readers find a solace of their own and empower them to
use their own voices, knowing they aren't alone.

> Almost 50% of all Black, Indigenous, and other people of color (BIPOC), as well as the LGBTQ+, suffer from mental health issues. This percentage has increased as a result of the COVID-19 crisis.

Loosen the Ties Which Bind Us to This Place and Commit to a Lighter Heart

By Niko Boskovic

How time drags on these sullen days
yet I am full of stories which ramble on in my head
spin out of control while slumbering
melt into reality like a seed newly sprouted
in soil not known for germination
but waiting for a tilling.

My favorite fantasy grips my attention every night.
In it I am not flying
nor am I quote-unquote normal
but rather, the world tilts to a precipitous angle and rights
    itself.
By rights itself, I mean it sheds
hate and guns and male toxicity and
violence in the name of peace.
It creates mothers in men
deepens our melanin to an umber hue
hastens love to our lips in place of meanness
makes the most macho of us humble
under the realization that we will all rot in the earth in one
    form or another someday.

Rake a path through September leaves
finish your weaving of songs with chores and
bend your old bones into the shape of a stream
that forks around life's current impasse
ready to float downstream to a quieter mind
where satisfaction is home
and life is still ripe with dreams of children.

Hang the laundry on the line of my smile until it dries
let me iron it to military stiffness
So you can wear it to church on Sunday
and sing as big as my dreams.

～

NEUROCLASTIC

A website of resources and articles built by a collective of Autistic people responsive to the evolving needs and trajectory of the Autistic community.

https://neuroclastic.com

How We Speak Our Truths

By Trini Feng

Two years ago, I barely touched social media. I only wandered to it every once in a while, scrolling through two weeks' worth of posts and dodging trends only because I was completely unaware they existed. I was going to school every day, talking to people every day, so I didn't see the need. For me, the couple of minutes I would spend talking in the hallways was enough social stimulation for a day. More, and I would quickly feel overwhelmed, caught in an ever-changing stream of interaction. Conversation always felt like art to me: delicate, easy to mess up with just one misstep. I always felt like I had to perfect every conversation with other people, so I'd interact sparingly.

Until, of course, that all disappeared. I think we're all well-acquainted with the feeling by now, the sudden snapping of the threads connecting us all. For a moment, I welcomed it. I've always kept to the edges of a crowd, never diving right into a conversation, so I thought this would be a worthwhile break. It was good, I thought, to move and not feel tied to someone else—like freedom, but freedom that wouldn't last forever.

I couldn't have known how long it was going to last, and I couldn't have known how that freedom would quickly make me begin to ache. The stream of conversation and connectedness had dried up, and I felt it then in the hoarseness of my throat. So I turned to the one thing I had always taken for granted: social media.

I had always been wary of social media. I had heard the rumors it was too polished, that everyone shared only the perfect moments of their life and easily buried their imperfections.

During the time I spent online before, I had seen that. But with the pandemic, my viewing habits changed. The posts I scrolled through edged closer to home. People were venting their own frustrations, their own pain, and they felt like mine, too. We all felt trapped, helpless, caught in some never-ending cycle, and screaming about it on social media—the only open place with other people—was our way of breaking those chains. Social media helped me feel less alone, to the point where I felt comforted around company rather than nervous.

From social media, I drifted to more personal online communities and servers. I found people I never imagined I would get the chance to talk to, people from all across the country and even from other countries. We bonded first over resentment, next over sorrow, then over sympathy. As we shared each of our situations, we sent each other hearts and cheerful GIFs, giving compassion when it was so hard to find. There was something unique about this form of communication: for the first time, I was talking with people who might look like me.

I've lived in the suburbs all my life. My neighborhood is quiet, peaceful, and incredibly white. I could count on my fingers the other Asian people in my school, and I rarely ever got the chance to talk with them. Online was different. I met so many BIPOC people, including other Asians like me, and they made me feel like I wasn't alone in a way I'd never experienced before.

When in-person events were shut down, I found myself reaching for something, anything else to fill the hole of interaction. And yes, online communication filled the void at first, but it grew beyond that. I confessed secrets about myself I hadn't before and realized truths to myself I hadn't quite connected. All the while, a supportive community stood behind me, encouraging me to continue growing and expressing my truth in all the ways that I wanted and deserved.

Of course, it wasn't the same as in-person communication. There are all the arguments against online communication: it can be fake, debilitating, rehearsed, and again, polished. To a degree, it's true, but especially during the height of the pandemic, that seemed to fall away.

We were all so isolated we needed someone to reach out to, and we didn't care about polishing ourselves. The friendships I made online in that time are bonds I want to keep forever. We were there for each other at our worst, and they taught me to climb up from that hole. I learned to be a better person. We taught each other about the world, sharing comments from other people that hurt us or the things we observed that cut even deeper.

Those conversations, more than anything else, showed me I have a duty to the people around me. Even if I don't understand their experience—especially if I don't—I want to make sure I show love above all. This comes with watching my boundaries, respecting labels, and most importantly, reaching out to make sure others feel comforted and at ease. While we were all stuck at home, I began practicing the ways in which I could be a better person to others. I learned where I stood in the world, and it was not to step over someone else, but to share my space with them and ask for mutual respect. I didn't have to create a perfect conversation like I always thought I had to. I just had to give the other person the respect that I wanted for myself. Slowly, with those reminders, I sought to put my nervousness at ease. I never stopped worrying about the right thing to say, but I did start telling myself it would be okay as long as the other person understood that I cared about them.

Eventually, those times of total isolation began to fade. Normal life crept back in with whatever limitations it held. Going back to school, especially, was a shock to my system.

Before the pandemic, it was yet another thing I took for granted, but now it seemed so difficult.

My school crowds fifteen hundred teenagers into a few hallways and a roundabout or two. Stepping into the building on the first day back felt like I had plunged headfirst into sensory disarray, competing with a thousand different stimuli from a thousand different directions. It was hard to feel completely at ease. I re-entered life more confident than I had been before, but there were still times when I wanted to shrink away, when there was so *much* happening I didn't know how to properly comprehend. Sometimes, I found myself reaching for the online communities I had discovered. At these times, I appreciated the slowness, the rehearsal of the messages we sent. It was a reprieve from the breakneck pace the rest of life had taken on, a refuge I could stretch and bask in. Online, I didn't have to struggle to keep up or stay in the moment as I sometimes did in-person. It was easier, in some ways, to breathe.

Slowly, I reconnected with the friends I had before the pandemic. I still enjoyed spending time with people face-to-face and communicating without delay. In-person, I was able to ramble on without worrying that I was taking up space. And seeing people react in live time to the things I said, being able to do the same for them, was a sort of dance I was eager to perform again because I knew the steps.

But it wasn't perfect. I may never forget the time my friend was joking about the "Chinese virus" while she sat across from me, a Chinese-American. At the time, I remembered the lessons I had learned in isolation, the respect I had told myself I would practice. I wondered, briefly, who else had done the same, who else had remembered there were still people different from them, even if they couldn't see them.

I can't say I was surprised. Again, my suburbs, though generally peaceful, have never been the most diverse. But the casual dismissal of it was something I had forgotten for a few months. I had been swept up in online trends, the movements led through hashtags and well-placed punctuation and emojis. Online, I couldn't go far without chancing upon a long passionate rant about the daily wrongs of life, the things we had to amend, and our hopes for the future. Everywhere I turned, an anonymous life's emotions would be on full display: rage, idealism, even simple hollowness. The pandemic took all of those emotions and sharpened them, forcing us to confront what simmered inside.

Since we've been drifting back to normalcy—or what we would consider a "normal" life—I still haven't found whether I also want to drift away from that emotional state. The truth is I liked the emotions rising out of me— emotions I hadn't confronted before. These were things I had held back for years, now spilling over because there was no reason to withhold them anymore. When flung back into face-to-face interactions, there was no longer much room for fervent emotions.

This often backfired online during the pandemic. If anyone said something problematic or hurtful, you could open a comment thread and see dozens of people pouncing on them. It could be incredibly toxic if it got out of control. But when those comments addressed the behavior rather than the person themselves, it was almost hopeful to see people standing up for what they believe in, forcing conversations, and not backing down. I was comforted knowing this wouldn't simply go ignored.

However in person, I retreated back into my shell. People threw around so many casual remarks no one could address all of them. Oftentimes, the best thing to do was ignore and move on—it was the most peaceful option, but it never sat well with me. I wanted to address what I felt was wrong. I wanted to be truthful to the people around me, and I wanted to help them become better. At the same time,

I wanted to be *around* other people. As much as I loved online communication, it wasn't a substitute for the two years of lacking in-person communication. But it was dangerous, too: my biggest fear is if I say one thing someone doesn't like, they will immediately distance themselves from me. Which seems a little extreme, and the actual chances of it happening are low, but I thought anything I said could hurt someone's feelings, break them apart. I wanted the people around me to feel respected and cared for, so much so that I was willing to let go of those ideas for myself. Every word made a difference between sweet and ignorant, kind and offensive, helpful and harmful. I would measure everything I said, debating whether my tone was just right to avoid offending someone in any way. I lived in a precarious balancing act that I performed for myself, agonizing over every word before I said it so I wouldn't worry even more after the fact.

But I'm slowly realizing I can't live like that forever. I can't fear criticizing someone else, much as I can't fear criticism from someone else. We're so closely interconnected with each other, we have to trust and help each other. Yet we're all such different people, and there will eventually be something we disagree on. But instead of judging the other person or fearing they will judge me, I want to have a conversation with them about it—a real one, so we can reconcile and welcome our differences. If I want someone to know I respect them, I have to be honest with them. Just because I call out someone's actions, it doesn't mean I don't care for them; far from it. I care enough and feel close enough that I think we can have a worthwhile conversation about our feelings.

The loneliness I felt in the pandemic has left me craving company, but I realize now that company isn't worth much if it's shallow. I've always wanted a "perfect" connection for myself, which I used to think was created by saying all the right things and never disagreeing with the other person. I worried that was the only way I could form lasting friendships with others and thought if there was ever an obstacle, the friendship would begin to decay. But I don't think a connection needs to be perfect more than it needs to bring us a little closer to perfection. I don't want to constantly worry about revealing my thoughts or others' ulterior motives. I'm going to start speaking my truth in whatever form it is. Whether it's perfect or not, I don't mind. I know that somewhere, whether in-person or online, someone will welcome my truth for what it is and fit it close to theirs.

∼

Author's Note: I wrote "How We Speak Our Truths" as a way to, well, speak my truth. Due to the pandemic, feelings of isolation were widespread everywhere, and everyone I knew was talking about how alone they had felt. I related deeply to what they felt, but I also felt that something was overlooked, namely in the new communities we had found online and the benefits they brought us. I wanted to discuss those new communities and how they affected my feelings of isolation. I also wanted to share my unique experience as a BIPOC during the pandemic.

I hope that whoever reads my piece is able to understand, in some way, my experiences and how the pandemic has affected everyone, including people that they are both similar to and different from. And I hope that somehow, by reading it, my audience feels less alone. It's hard to feel connected in times like these, but hopefully, my piece helps bring people together.

Consequence of Culture

By Genevieve Bascos-Arce

RULE 2.
study.
You must be smart.

RULE 3.
FLOAT
You must not drown.
A good girl solves her own problems.

RULE 4:
SWIM
The water is actually quite comfortable.

RULE 5:
BE THE DIFFERENCE
Enough wallowing. Might as
well enjoy it :.

~

Author's Note: The mind shackles the body at birth. Eye shape, skin color, and height are aspects that embody one's individuality. One plus one equals two, and ethnicity plus culture equals a hundred. Given Asian culture, you must meet expectation after expectation. The consequence of the unstated curriculum consists of three rules you must follow to meet the deadlines and satisfy the greed to grow. If the rules break, you will drown from the disappointment that seeps into your lungs.

Once you establish a way to overcome rules one through three, I suppose you will understand that you cannot run from the traits embedded in your person. Ethnicity plus culture equals a hundred, so you might as well add them to the equation and learn to thrive.

> We need to take care of our minds as much as we need to take care of our bodies. We do not have to be in a bad place before we reach out for help.

Part III

The Journey Continues

Fault

By Keona Burch

It was a stupid fight
Just one of too many
I can't even remember the words
Only the sage walls, the computers, the books
And your face
Red and blotchy because I made you cry

This isn't the first time you'd leave
suddenly and silently
No one knows where you drive
And no one knows when you'll get back
All I know is the forest green car
disappears down the road
And I know better than to ask for answers

Dad reassures me you are safe
But I do not know whether to believe him
And I do not know if he believes himself
All I know is to continue
Pretend you aren't absent
Sleep with the emptiness
of the storms brewing
You are always back by morning
I do not know how I find it
if you left it open

or gave it to me
or told me

I only have bits and pieces
of blurry memories
blunt documents, your voice, your tears
But I can feel your message
It doesn't matter how I got it
Just that I knew

You thought you'd failed me
That you were a bad mom
That I was better without you
I let you down
I wasn't good enough to make you happy
I was the nuisance, the burden, the failure
And I was hurting you

I was too young to understand suicide
But darkness is magnetic

You got help climbing out
But I pulled myself up, because
You couldn't know I had fallen
You would only blame yourself

That is why I hold you
while your sobs twist my heart
How I know what to say when you are sad
Why I hide the pain I'm facing
How I learned to cry silent and alone
You shouldn't worry about me

That is why I work harder
Strive for perfection
Tell you my successes
So you can be proud of your daughter

So you can know
I am everything I am
because of you

~

EMBRACE RACE

Embrace Race was founded by two parents who set out to create a community and gather resources for challenges faced by those raising children in a world where race matters.

The 5 Stages of Grief: A Map of the Mind
By Kaitlyn O'Neill

I now stand before *denial*
With tears in my eyes, cold and bitter,
And confusion in my heart
I try to wake up but to no avail
Overwhelmed and overloaded with emotions
A defense mechanism for the soul
The trip is cruel yet inevitable
But I have a ways to go

Welcome to *anger*
I am met with gates of rage and wrath
I stop dead in my tracks
Ambushed with feelings I can't control
That same bitter taste washes over my mouth as
The pain firmly grasps me
Like a humiliating chokehold, a relentless illness
It infects my actions and taunts my mind
But while the fury subsides,
I'm snatched, only to break down again

Here awaits *bargaining*
A bitter negotiation of pain and sadness
My tear-stained face looks for answers
In efforts to regain what I had,

I fear losing it once again
I convince myself it can be done
While the universe mocks what is already gone
A delicate dam to delay the incoming waves of sorrow and
    guilt

I make my way to *depression*
The most lonesome and desolate point in my journey
I feel the cold air encase my body
And reluctantly feel it seep into my brain
Coerced to be vulnerable in my hazy state of mind
A shade of navy-blue glasses, cover my eyes
Turning every cheerful greeting into a grievous memory
And each interaction I have into a tragic exchange
I feel the emotional weight, it almost seems physical at this
    point
But the end is so near, I must continue, I must
I must

And I arrive at *acceptance*
Greeted with a faint breeze carrying hope,
That caresses my face and wipes dry my tears
A final destination of my bitter embrace
I have come to terms with how unfair it has been
But I recognize that life must go on
Loss is never easy, but a hard hit to the soul and its well-
    being
Whether it's for forever or not
I've traveled a long and painful path
Filled with too many reactions and sentiments to count

But alas

I have made it.

~

Author's Note: I wrote, "The 5 Stages of Grief: A Map of the Mind" in hopes I could share my perspective on emotional development during a time many of us have experienced, especially throughout the pandemic. My aim is that the people who read and listen to the poem find a sense of comfort and they are never alone in their journey of grief. My goal was to translate these difficult emotions we often can't explain to others into a piece of poetry that resonates with the larger community. Whether it's the loss of a loved one or just a rough patch in someone's life, this poem is for anyone and everyone who needs it.

Gratitude Practice is a coping strategy for mental health:

1) Notice Good Things
2) Start a Journal
3) Soak It Up
4) Express Yourself
5) Do Something Kind

Painting by Freya Sticka

Nothing

By Freya Sticka

"And I said,
Mama, are these walls real?
Mama, are the windows really clear?
Hush, hush. The sun is only rising.
Mama, mama, the sun doesn't hear the footsteps in my
    chest
Hush, hush. Your breath is as warm as the summer rays.
Mama, ma! I'm in the shade.
Hush, hush. How could you be so distant? You're right here.
Ma, ma. I don't know.
Hush.
Ma, I can't feel my skin.
Hush, it simply isn't there.
Ma, has it ended?
Already has.
Ma, please, I'm not here yet.
Ma, take me home.
Ma, please, I really don't know.
Mama, please. I don't know a thing.
Mama, I am but a child.
Yet your body has grown?
I don't know.
Is it really just me in this world?'
Maybe.
Hm?

Not even you are in this world.
You're not my ma.

. . .

Who are you?
Why does that matter?
Who are you?
I am you.
But you said there is no me?
Yes.

. . .

Who am I?
Depends.
I don't know.

. . .

I have no body. No brain. No heart.
Maybe.
There is nothing?
No, there is nothing.
I don't understand?
Not even nothingness can exist in this world.

. . .

The sun is setting.
I don't want to leave yet.
What could you be leaving?
What do you mean?
There is nothing left in this world for us.
What about the walls? The windows?

What walls? What windows?

There was no reply. None was needed. For this silence is who I am, why I am. It is why the windows, walls, sync the footsteps in their chest with mine.

Our bodies are not who we are, simply what defines who we are. Our thoughts and emotions are not who we are, simply what paves who we are. Who are we? We are the witness, the spirit.

Before I knew it, the sun had set.

Everything was no longer nothing, nor something.

YOUTH.GOV

youth.gov is the U.S. Government website that helps you create, maintain, and strengthen effective youth programs. Included are youth facts, resources and evidence-based youth programs.

A Wish for Rain

By Keona Burch

I say it's my middle name. It's a joke, a self-deprecating dig, a "bet you can't pronounce my name."

I win.

They try. They try, but they can never quite fit the awkward syllables into their mouths, stumbling over them as if they were the jutting roots on hiking trails, worn thin but precarious.

I say that it's my middle name.

It's not. My middle name is a husk, carved hollow by foreign fingers, where *Jade Emperor* and *Rain Flute* are the same. It is not empty, sharp, cumbersome, jagged. It is not the echoing scrape of sabre blades, or the smashing of their guards.

It is missing my mom's surname. Zhāng. She holds it close, fighting stubbornly against the society that pressures her to change.

She did not do the same for me.

My name is built on an uneven middle, five thousand kilometers farther from one dusty half. It is not who I am. It is not the magnificent cities of ice, the bustling chaos and noise, the knowledge my ancestors were proud of.

It is not where I'm from.

哈尔 上海 第十一楼的公寓

My name is the one secure connection, bridging me to two separate worlds. The last reminder that I belong to Chinese family gatherings, where they speak to me in fluent Mandarin. I can only respond in short fragments.

好

我很喜欢

谢谢

I'm missing too many pieces of the puzzle
We are family, and we can barely communicate past superficial greetings or instructions.
We are family, and I cannot write their names.
They are where I am from.

马泽，激雷，劲松，云笛，竑烨，丽春，澍械，张

My names represent two halves of me, but neither acknowledges the other. One sits like an ornament, displayed only to prove something to someone, once in a blue moon.

In English, my name means 'God's gracious gift,' a present from a God none of us believe in.

My name is Hawaiian. My family is not. I don't pronounce my name right, no one does. But it is fields of flowers on warm, summer days, bright as glittering gemstones. It is the melody of a family laughing together, as light and joyful as the cloud-made shapes drifting across the sky.

In Chinese, my name is the soft, airy melody of the flute, the ones I was named after. It is the stable petrichor on crisp, dewy mornings, the roar or the crystal blue dragons, and the gentle flow of rivers.

Keona Burch 张雨笛

I have two names, but only one is used. The other is forgotten, like the home and the language that made it, nine thousand miles away.

∽

Author's Note: While I have used writing as a way to process my emotions for a while, I never considered writing poetry until recently. This year in English class, I learned a lot about poetry. The countless forms of poetry appealed to me, and since then, I have enjoyed writing with less rigid rules. My main motivation for sharing these poems is to help other people feel less alone. While you are struggling with identity or mental health, it is very easy to feel isolated. With these poems, I hope to reassure other people that they are not alone and encourage them to reach out when they need help. I would like to thank my parents for supporting me and my English teacher, Pat, for always making time to help me improve my writing.

Singularity

By Katherine Elliott

What makes someone human?
I am a person with no real defining personality traits, or
    excessive talents.
I am like a shadow in the back of the room; everyone knows
    I'm there, but nobody acknowledges my presence.
The chair beside me is empty.
Many, many times I've seen that,
The emptiness threatens to swallow me whole,
consuming my thoughts and
filling me with nothingness, and yet everything at once.
The tangle of unspoken words gnawing
in the back of my mind, clawing
to make itself known.
Even so, I can't open my mouth to speak because nobody
    will listen. Or maybe, they're the ones
covering my mouth without my knowing.
I want to know, have you become someone like me?

Maybe it's a silent apartment,
or an empty seat at the table.
I know how it feels!
It's quite ironic isn't it,
so many lonely people now, but the Earth is overpopulated.
These thoughts only come when I'm at the desk, hunched
    over, panicked eyes working across the room, frantically
    darting back and forth to make sure "they" are not
      watching
      staring
      judging

seeing
me,
all of me . . .
me as a person, because sometimes I just don't want to be
   seen.
Me, because I have never fit in with the Emmas and Rachels
   and Kristines
with their porcelain skin
and bright blonde hair,
but i know i don't belong
With the other Filipino kids
who always left me out
and the grandmas who stare at me in the store
whispering something i will never know
but never forget.

. . . why couldn't I have learned my own
language? why did i have to be born in half
life forever a conflict, a *divide* between worlds
I swallow the forming lump in my throat,
the one clawing its way into my mouth,
threatening to spill over
and
drown me
in my own tears.

Sometimes, you think
everything around you is collapsing,
the stability of life crumbling
and you just can't take it anymore.
Lamenting about your life problems is not going to fix
   anything. You'll get pity from the ones who are kind, but
   never seem to be there
when you need someone the most.

You are a mirror, reflecting and helping others recognize
     themselves, but never truly getting to have a voice
     yourself.
Resolution?
The best and most honorable actions of one never get
     attention or praise.
And if you need to be reminded,
sometimes it's okay to cry
sometimes it's okay to have feelings
and sometimes,
sometimes it's okay
to not be okay.

no matter how many times you are pushed down,
always get back up.
not because you want recognition,
but instead to let others know they're not alone, either. all
     humans are born with natural hatred towards others,
but it's up to you
whether or not to overcome hatred
with the goodness inside.

~

Author's Note: I made this work to show the struggle of
constantly feeling isolated and the Imposter syndrome of
being mixed. I hope my audience can sympathize with my
piece and hopefully some will feel less alone knowing that
many people can feel the same way, especially during the
pandemic. A lot of people, including my peers at school
would definitely feel connected to this writing and I think
that's why it should be shared. I had spoken to my friends
about how they felt and it influenced me. Thanks to my
mom, sister and grandparents who were also an inspiration
and continue to encourage me.

You Matter

You Matter is a safe space for youth to discuss and share stories about mental health and wellness, including Anxiety, Depression, and Eating Disorders.

Zitkala Sa Winyan

By KyLynn Lucio

Growing up is not always an easy thing. I've watched many coming-of-age movies that made me think growing up would be amazing. But the maturing I had to do at an early age says otherwise, because my childhood wasn't the absolute best. But that doesn't mean it was horrible, so let me explain.

My mom was a teen mom. She was learning as I was learning. I loved every single moment with my mom. All those memories led to the healthy relationship we have now. I love to refer to my mom as not only my mom but my best friend. My mother was always there for me. She is still there for me. I appreciate her a lot. The only truly bad thing was she taught me to be perfect. I think that is why I am so hard on myself to this day.

I can't really blame her for my perfectionism. She was young and doing everything on her own.

My dad was a deadbeat father. He will never know about being a good parent because he was barely ever a parent to begin with. But there were times he would come into my life for a short amount of time. I was a huge daddy's girl. I loved my dad so much, I thought he was the best dad in the world because he was, when he was present. But then he would leave before the holidays came. When he left, I felt sad because that's when I needed him most. Now that I am older, I don't need him because my mom is so amazing at being a single mother.

Being Native American, we lived with our family, so she got help and support from my grandparents, uncles, and my auntie. I was always with my grandparents when I was young. I remember always going to the store or going to get McDonalds. I loved being with them. I also loved being with my auntie and uncles. I would play Barbies with my uncle Gaylon and my auntie Taylor. I remember my auntie made a Barbie house out of fabric drawers and I was so amazed. My uncle Gaylon would grab a blanket and style it on me like a dress. I would go to the end of the hall and model it for him. My uncle Warren used to play guitar and I wanted to be just like him so I got a toy guitar with Disney princesses on it from Walmart. I loved to play it and sing too. My uncles built Barbie houses and scooters from Walmart for me.

I was an only child until my brother Takoja came three years after me. So a lot of the attention was focused on me and him. I think it was good for me though because it distracted me and my brother from the bad happening around us.

Sometimes my auntie and uncles would go buy alcohol and when they drank too much, they were bad drunks. There were arguments and fights. They really scared me; I was so confused and young. I barely had any idea what was going on. But they were teaching me I don't want to be like that. I think everything happens for a reason.

The things that traumatized me, like the drunken fights and my dad leaving, happened for a reason. The drunken fights were showing me what alcohol can do to you. Especially being Native American, drinking and doing drugs is a horrible idea overall, since Native Americans suffer most from alcohol and drug addictions. I am so proud of the Natives who are recovering from addiction. I have never done alcohol or drugs and I don't plan to, as we are breaking generational cycles. I am glad I get to teach my younger siblings and cousins the right path. I can help lead them to the red road. The red road, in Native culture, is the positive and sacred path. It's basically the 'good' path of life.

I am the oldest of all my siblings and cousins. I have four siblings (in order) they are Takoja, Hayden, Samia, and Tokala. I don't live with Hayden and I barely see him because we have different moms but the same dad. Takoja means "grandchild" in my language, he is thirteen years old currently. Samia is just a name my mom loved because it's kind of like her name, Sammi.

Samia is five years old and looks like my mini me. Tokala means "fox" in my language. Tokala is two years old and he looks like a mini Tako (Tako is Takoja's nickname). I love my siblings so much. I hope I am a good role model for them.

I prioritize school and my mental health so I can hopefully be that good role model. I plan to graduate and go to college to be a teacher, a therapist, or a writer. I would love to teach young children art or something. I would also love to be a therapist to help people with their mental health. I am huge about good mental health because of everything I have been through. My childhood was good, but there were a couple bumpy roads. But then, getting closer to the teenage years, I was first sexually violated and it was by my own cousin. I was so confused about what she was doing. But I knew I felt disgusted with her, myself, and my body.

The second time I was sexually violated was 2020 and by my boyfriend of a year. I knew what was happening this time. But both times, I felt as if someone died. Like a part of me died every time it happened. Nobody knew about it the first time because I didn't completely understand it.

But the second time, I told my family and my therapist about four months after it happened. The second time was ten times worse. I put my whole trust into that boy, and he betrayed me. This took a huge toll on me and my mental health. I felt, depressing, not me. Recently I was assaulted for the third time. February 26th, 2022, the day my life changed completely. It was not a long relationship before this boy assaulted me. We dated for two to three weeks. It destroyed me completely. It was exactly one year and two months after I was assaulted the second time. I felt broken. I wanted to die. That night I came home and I was alone. My family had gone to my grandparents without me. I felt alone and I was having deep emotions I had never imagined. I was angry, sad, depressed, suicidal, shocked, and alone. It was the worst night of my life. I felt like I had just lost myself to the darkness.

The next morning, I told my grandma and my mom what he did to me. Not only did he affect me, he affected my whole family. We all hugged each other and cried. I started missing school a lot because he went to my school and had my same classes. I couldn't even find myself to get up in the morning. All I could think about was what he did to me. So my mom told the school caseworker. I was then forced to report the incident. I wasn't ready for this. I was trying to process all my feelings and I already had to report it two days later. I was angry but I knew it was what had to be done. A detective came into my home and questioned me about what happened that night; this was very traumatizing. The detective would ask me "What time was that around?"

I would tell him I didn't know. I'm a teenager, I don't care about the time unless I have to be somewhere at a specific time and place. I got the reason he needed to know timing but I had to answer these kinds of questions so many times. Now, whenever I hang out with my friends or with a guy I look at the time at least every ten minutes. I am scared of being violated again. I trust only a small circle of people.

Both of my recent assaults (second and third time), I was harassed by someone mutual or related to my abuser. The second time, when I started to use my voice, his friends called me a liar. They told me that my abuser would never hurt me. They said I was mad because he cheated on me. In fact, I was glad he cheated because I loved him too much to leave him. So I'm glad he left me instead. The third time I was assaulted, my abuser's mom harassed me. I worked at my local market as a cashier and she came in the Monday after they received my restraining order against her son, my abuser. She told me to stop messaging her son. I wasn't messaging her son at all. I didn't plan on messaging him either. I was just raped by him. I didn't want to keep contact.

That's the whole reason I got a restraining order against him! When she confronted me, her breath was on me. She was close, very close. My coworkers told her to leave and my managers told me to go to the office. So I did and I ended up going home and reporting her.

A week or two later, we had a court hearing because she didn't want a harassment restraining order against her. Especially because I worked at the only local market. I understood, but my safety was my priority. She kept making excuses like if I was working and there was an emergency. Even the judge was annoyed. We had to do a second court hearing. This time, she got what she wanted. The harassment restraining order was taken down. I screamed crying after the zoom meeting. I did not feel safe working at my local market anymore, so I put in my two weeks' notice. She hasn't harassed me since but I still have my worries about if I see her.

To backtrack a bit, I didn't have good friends like I do now. During spring 2021, I was healing and processing the second assault. My friends then were not helpful. They would invalidate my feelings when I tried to open up to them. They were not understanding at all and thought I was making it all about me. This sucked because I wanted friends who would support me. But I had my family and my therapist supporting me. I learned that friends are not forever. Even during my childhood, girls on the rez were so mean to me. In elementary school I had only one real friend.

His name was Keech. He moved away before middle school so I was back to having no real friends. Throughout middle school and high school, these girls continued to call me names and give me bad looks. I would sometimes even go home crying to my mom and my grandma. But now I just feel bad for them. I think it was mostly because they were jealous of me and my family.

My family is Oglala Lakota, from Pine Ridge, SD, and we value the Lakota way. Which, my grandma tells me, is love, kindness, honesty, and respect. We have much love for our family and our people. I think the teenage years are about learning about yourself and growing into who you are going to be. But so far, mine have been about losing myself and starting over again. I have had so many setbacks while being young. I am learning to heal from all of it. But healing is a lifelong journey. It does get a bit exhausting from time to time. But I would rather be here than not.

My outlet from all of this was poetry, writing, reading, and learning about astrology and zodiac signs. When I read poetry by Rupi Kaur, I felt so inspired. She writes about so much stuff that I can relate to. Rupi Kaur writes about mental health, assault, and also her culture. One of my favorite quotes from Rupi Kaur: "despite knowing they won't be here for long they still choose to live their brightest lives—*sunflowers*" pg. 91 of "The Sun and Her Flowers." This is one of my favorites because my family nickname used to be Sunshine. Not only that but it gave me reason to not be so down about the things I went through. I learned that I can be happy while healing.

But Rupi Kaur has definitely helped me in so many ways. It's so crazy to me because she doesn't even know me! She is my role model. I would love to be like her someday. Here are some of the things I have written while taking care of my mental health:

- The crowd doesn't see depression, the crowd sees stuck up, angry, irresponsible, and disrespectful.

- We were literally beauty and the beast, but in reverse; happy beginnings, horrible ending.

- Unbreaking my own broken heart is difficult. Especially because I'm not at fault for it breaking.

- I'm so happy they left me. I would have never left them because I never knew how horrible I let them treat me. It was so bad that I had so much insecurities and loss of self-worth. I doubted myself so much while being surrounded by these bad influences. I'm so happy that they are gone. I'm so happy with my life without them. They love to bring up the past and that's how I know that I'm the mature and bigger person. I am able to understand experiences and learn from them. I genuinely do learn from these life lessons and I am grateful to be.

- I used to dwell on that I should've known but I wouldn't have known unless I went through it. I did go through those hard experiences but everything happens for a reason.

Something I can learn from this is that there can always be a positive outlook on things, even in the bad.

～

Author's Note: I have been through a lot in my lifetime. Even though I am still young and currently fifteen years young. Since I have been through so much, I feel that I could be the person who can give support to someone who needs it. What other better way is there than to write about my life! In my essay, I talk about very deep and emotional events. It was hard to write about those things but it was so that people like me won't feel alone. You are not alone, there are people around you who care!

After being assaulted, I was forced to be quarantined because of Covid-19. This isolation made it so much more difficult for me. I was more depressed and failing my classes on distance learning because I had no motivation to do schoolwork. I felt that I couldn't get help because I felt that I was misunderstood by everyone. I wasn't as close with my family and friends like I used to be.

But in reality, I was mentally isolating myself from everyone because I was already physically isolated. I didn't tell anyone about what I went through until summer was getting closer. After I told people, I felt so much weight come off from my chest. I felt so loved and lifted. I feel that way every time that I tell someone about my trauma. This is why my essay is important! I want to inspire some of my readers to do the same as I did! I want you all to begin your healing! I am not saying you should tell everyone about your trauma but I am saying that if coloring or showering makes you feel better, I say do it! Healing is a lifetime process, be patient with yourself. I feel that mental health is not talked about enough. Mental health is normal! I would not have learned this if it wasn't for my beautiful *iná* (mom in Lakota). I am so proud and thankful for my mom; she has gone through so much. But regardless she has shown up for me and my siblings every single day. I love my mom so much because I know that not everyone can say that about theirs.

RAINN.ORG

RAINN is the nation's largest anti-sexual violence organization.

Chat online at online.rainn.org OR call 1-800-656-4673

Lost

By Erik Nielsen

1

I walked, then stopped, and looked about the street,
With nothing gripping my gaze on concrete
My body's own soul left behind my feet,
My mind, it was split, but my thoughts, complete.

I didn't leave much in that appalling place,
Indeed I wouldn't think twice to go erase
The worthless words or wishes that my own face
Had written on this solitary space.

Back then, I needed not care for a thing,
Youth blinded me from sorrows that life bring,
Which follow me everywhere I go, and cling;
Now, mem'ries of my earlier days sting.

As pains from my past are hard to discuss,
Discussing the past seems superfluous.

Lost! Mistakes surround me,
Silent! For none can hear my plea,
Battle-scarred! Forlorn while waiting for thee.

2

Woes of my past took time away, but not grief;
I'd sit around consid'ring what couldn't change,

I stole time from myself; I was the thief;
While thoughts of stealing from myself seem strange,
I couldn't shake my subconscious, odd belief:
The past lives to destroy and disarrange.

My life's been backwards e'er since I was born;
As I was trying to escape the maze,
I caught myself on thicket and its thorn,
Its end obscured from my befuddled gaze.

Alone, attempting to chart my own path,
If only you could be here to guide me;
The past invokes its unforgivable wrath,
That time is gone, lost deep down in the sea.

Lost! In my maze of life,
Silent! I can't hear over strife,
Battle-scarred! Life stabbed me with its cruel knife.

3

My life could be delightful, I suppose,
Be brightened by its poems and its prose,
Be happy 'till my days come to a close,
And be content with everything I chose.

On what could have been, I'd rather not dwell,
Instead escaping from my lonely cell,
No silence now, for others hear me yell,
"I've overcome the past! Doubts I dispel!"

For once, it all makes sense to me; at last!
I lived not for today, but for the past,

I needed help, when I could've nicely asked,
I mourned instead, while my gift of time passed.

Those days are gone, just like my days of youth,
Tomorrow is a new day filled with truth.

From time to time, our mem'ries we allow,
But, past is gone and present is right now.

Author's Note: We've all had that time when we've just felt lost. Even talking to the people who care about you doesn't feel right so instead we let our feelings suffocate inside of us. While reading Auden's "Musee des Beaux Arts," I realized that suffering goes on around me all the time, and it's really easy to feel like you're alone in your suffering when nobody else wants to talk about what they are going through.

Especially in the world that we live in now, it's easier than ever to disconnect from others and lose yourself in the past. Through my art, I want to urge people to stay in the present and appreciate the gift of life we're given every day.

DOMESTIC VIOLENCE HOTLINE

If you or a loved one is in a situation that feels unsafe, you can call 1-800-799-SAFE or text START to 88788.

My Mental Health Journey

By Mila Kashiwabara

Hi, I'm Mila and I'm ten years old!

Lately I have not been feeling like myself. At the most random times I start bursting into tears. I have an urge to clench my fists and just want to hit something. I say "I can't, I can't, I can't" and I don't know what I can't do I just know I can't do anything. I don't know how I see hope in all that darkness but I do know that my mom always tells me I'm okay and that I'll get through it.

But I also like to read an enthusiastic book called Friends Forever. It is based on the author's life in eighth grade. Throughout the book it shows her trying to be perfect or beautiful but at the end she comes to the realization she just needs to be enough for herself. We also see her go through a lot of depression. The book shows me that I am not alone and that gives me hope.

I know I would help a friend or loved one. I just don't know how. I have not had a lot of friends going through anxiety, fear or them being stressed out. I am aware one of my friends is always very stressed out with things like homework and getting things done in time. When things like that happen to her I decide to leave her alone. I just need to let her do her homework and cool down. I give her the gift of space and respecting her feelings. But if it seems like someone is sad I would usually try to cheer them up. In these cases I think this would be the most helpful thing.

I actually go through anxiety myself. Sometimes I have a fear of running out of oxygen. And I always get very anxious if I do not have my water bottle with me. I have panic attacks and get shortness of breath. At first I thought it was a medical issue. But whenever I did not have my water bottle on hand, the bad things I thought would happen never happened. Since my mom is a psychologist I knew a little bit about what anxiety was. My mom saying she was worried about me made me worry. It took me a little over a year to come to the realization that I might need some help controlling my anxiety.

My mom thought it was a good idea for me to get a therapist and so did I. I had thought it would be really awkward but I knew my mom knew what she was doing. It took us a while but then we found the perfect therapist for me. Since I am a person of color (Asian and Latina) it was important to have a therapist of color as well. And we had not seen any. I was a little worried, but we ended up finding a great therapist who is Asian like me. Although I was a little scared and embarrassed at first because I was going to tell someone I didn't really know things I had never told anyone. Plus there have always been stereotypes in shows and in books that taking therapy was bad and humiliating. Also hearing people making jokes about it didn't help at all. But she ended up being great. She has given me a lot of tips about my anxiety that has really helped. So I learned that therapy really does do something, and I am very grateful.

∼

Author's Note: I wrote this piece around a year ago and a lot has changed. For example I no longer say "I can't" over and over again, but I still go through anxiety. When I look back on this piece, I hope that I have helped people feel heard and not alone.

Ripped from the Arms of Logic and Knocking on the Neighbor's Door for the Spare Key

By Niko Boskovic

This rain is the alarm I need on this first day after the
    holidays when routines return and the world feels
    like nothing changed.
Except it did.
Somewhere between Christmas and New Year's
my great sense of calm was replaced with an urgency
to fix and straighten everything I could.

My OCD is a raging bull that wakes at dawn
and doesn't relent until I fall asleep.
The beast won't ever rest
even when I am exhausted
its eyes are covered and caked
in the stadium's dust.
Even when I relax
the bull scrapes its hooves in preparation
of a charge at any friendly face.

It doesn't hear the fatigue in my father's voice
or the fury in my sister's yell as she tries to interrupt my
    ritual.

It gets enraged by their words that fall like blossoms
from the three cherry trees that line our front yard
every spring dusting our cars in a festivity reminiscent
of a Hindu wedding.
Then, forgotten like a drunken argument between
          lovers they eventually return to affection.

But the bull keeps a tally
of every spear thrust with bloodlust
into the space between its shoulders
a pit so deep and rent with scars
that blades don't penetrate.
How many blades have tried!

I know someday one will push its way into that gap
where my OCD curls up to sleep
and with a measured flick of the wrist
it will die
going slowly to a place
where such things are buried
and I will no longer feel its intense hold on my life.

Soon, in a matter of time
(if measured by billable hours)
I will be free from all these unseeable urges
to let my decisions form like drops of rain
and fall from the prettiest clouds.

～

OCD IN KIDS

This website has a directory and resources for kids and parents. It includes therapists, clinics, support groups, and organizations specializing in helping children with OCD.

Bent and Broken

By Veronica Salrin

The bed sinks as I lie, relieving the weight from the day, I lie
    awake with sparks in my skull and spines in my sides.
Wondering, weeping, whispering, "What did I do to deserve
    this?" yelling out to any higher power.
Whoever is willing to listen to the bent and broken.

Mornings full of mourning,
Longing for the life I once led,
Yet wanting to love the one I lead.
Complications and confusion crowding my cranium:
Is my brain bent and broken as well?

Both arms are tied to two thoughts.
The executioner shoots, the thoughts pull,
Tearing me up inside, and tearing up my eyes.
Bent and broken, and bashing my own brain.
Just for being her beautiful self.

Stuck in my tracks,
The ground beneath my feet is honey.
Contrarily, though I am stuck,
I feel more at home than ever.
A pretty and pristine perspective,
I wish I could live in its hue.
Cover me, oh liquid gold,

Sickeningly sweet, stolen from your comfortable hive.
Fallen to my knees, I shove the feelings way back in the
    dark,
Inside the cold cabinets, filled with the deepest secrets
The deepest thoughts, the biggest lies,
And now, how I feel about myself deep down,
Bent and broken, but putting on a fixed face.

Acceptance accelerates, but I still struggle,
Walking becomes harder and harder,
More painful, as though my joint sockets are sandpaper.
Rubbing down whatever is left,
Of the bent and broken me.
Each reminder of pain pulls me down,
I cover myself in the syrup
beneath me putting on that positive perspective
That makes the bent and broken attractive again.

I am everything but simple, and everything but honest,
Fine doesn't describe me, but what am I expected to say?
Watching people cramming towards me
Wishing to aid me, help me, fix me.
That's what the bent and broken are for,
Not for their own lives, but to assist others in theirs,
"Look at me," their actions cry
"She needed me, she's bent and broken"

I'm independent, and needy,
I'm in pain, yet sometimes I thrive,
I'm doing fine, yet barely holding on,
I'm empathetic, yet blunt,

Truly a walking contradiction.
As the bent and broken often are.

When the yellow sun sets for the final time,
Greeting the blue night, for the last time.
I return to the beginning, and I lay my sweet head down
The angels that have been watching me wipe my tears,
Death does not sadden me as much as the thought
Of inconveniencing others, upsetting others, leaving others.

As the women in white lift me, I'm reassured,
But far too late, they fear,
I lived my life covering up my feelings of being bent and
     broken
To not hurt others.
Neglecting the truths that I should've accepted; I hid it all
     beneath.
Wake up, wake up! I tell myself,
Being bent and broken isn't all there is,
Yet I don't need to hide it.
Maybe I can be something new.
I can be beautiful and beaming instead.

~

Author's Note: Living with Hypermobility Spectrum
Disorder means many things for me. It means living with
constant hidden pain, having to give up the things you love,
and being misunderstood by peers and doctors. I want my
audience to know that they aren't alone in feeling broken
due to a disorder or disability. My struggles started around
the pandemic, and the isolation felt from both the pandemic
and my disability caused a plethora of mental struggles. It

felt like I couldn't tell people about my disability without either being pitied or joked about. I think the most important thing about my work is solidarity, knowing that I am not the only one who feels broken due to things I cannot control. I want to share it to give other people hope about their circumstances, because I know what it feels like to feel isolated and broken.

WELLNESS RECOVERY ACTION PLAN

Discover simple, safe, effective tools to maintain wellness and develop a plan to keep moving forward so you can gain support and stay in control.

Taken for Granted

By Kaitlyn O'Neill

For the past two years, I took it for granted
I'll admit,
I took *it* for granted
It being the friendly greetings in the hall
It being the smiles on faces too familiar to forget
It being the hustle and bustle of crowded streets under
    sunlit clouds
It being the delicate touch and physical energy of others
It being the group photos with messy hair and imperfect
    smiles,
The sense of security in our communities bonded by steel
    made cables,
And finding comfort in the presence of people who make up
    the mechanics of our memories
Yet we rarely stop to think,
Think about what we've lost and endured
But "lost" isn't simply something misplaced,
Rather the experiences never to be had, the forgotten joy of
    others, and the people we can never get back
And "endured" can never hold the weight of how we
    survived on LED-lit screens, mental health so fractured
    that a broken vase seems more put together, and
    periods of isolation spanning eons
As time went on, pieces of my life began to chip away,

Like how a sandcastle breaks down upon the shore,
Waves take their course and wither away the sand
Trying so hard to stay together despite the harsh wind and
    crashing waves
The tower, once tall, dwindles down to nothing more than
    an abandoned pile,
But despite cracks, crevices, uneven arches, and slanted
    walls
We still rebuild
Our once uneven arches become sturdy and solid
Our slanted walls become adorned with beauty and hope
Our days spent inside become days spent with friends
Our anxiety-ridden worry eased by the safety nets of
    people we love
Our socially starved selves welcome the physical contact of
    others with open arms
What was once a majestic palace, fallen, only to be
    reconstructed again
Now, as we find ourselves discovering this new "normal"
Filled with those familiar faces, crowded spaces, hugs, and
    handshake
We can't help but appreciate the world a little more,
The transformation of our lives, but this time for the better
Almost as the world blooms from the remains of isolated
    dust
Blooms from strides as a community
Blooms from our strength
Blooms from what we've lost
Blooms from our hope

Blooms into the world we are rediscovering, one step at a
    time

And I will never take it for granted again.

~

Author's Note:　　My poem "Taken for Granted" was
initially designed as a part of a local dance project and
performance. While writing it, I wanted to take on multiple
factors of what challenged so many of us during the
pandemic. I intended to bring awareness to parts of my life
I had taken for granted and hadn't realized up until now.
Through sharing perspectives on mental health struggles to
overwhelming isolation, I hope this poem can connect with
readers and listeners who share the same bittersweet
memories I do from these past two years.

ACTIVE MINDS

Active Minds is the nation's premier nonprofit organization supporting mental health awareness and education for young adults.

Good Kid

By Danica Leung

You ask any parent around me growing up,

and the answer is the same.

Academic overachiever,
extracurricularly excellent,
a Forbes 30 under 30 in the rough.

But that can't be right.

Can it?

REC
Because when people ask:
How you holding up, kiddo? You doing good?
they're not asking about my resume.
They mean, if I'm doing well.
If I can get out of bed.
If I keep myself fed.
If I can escape my own head.
CAM 7

And what you're supposed to say is:
Yeah.
Yeah, I'm– I'm good.
No matter what.

Never mind the fact that at this moment --
I'm not.
Not in any sense of the word.

So I allow myself to not be good.
sniff

To not
be okay.

sob
The world cannot
ask for more than
today's attempt
at wellness --
no matter how unsuccessful.

The first question I asked when starting therapy was:
How do I know when I am better?

Now I know the answer.
STARTING ROUTE

It's my ability to gather my limbs,
and courage,
and whatever else is left of me,

and to lay myself bare
to the wonders of the world.
Fin.

Author's Note: I rediscovered the poem "Wild Geese" by Mary Oliver during a college application preparation session. The lady counseling us on how to optimize our SAT scores and extracurriculars prefaced the Zoom call with the poem as a frame of reference — to get some perspective on how small college apps were, in the grand scheme of things.

I ended up taking that advice to heart. I had plenty of time during the pandemic to reflect, and so I reflected: what was the point of running the rat race, in the end? What did I want to do with my life? Did any of it matter?

Getting back to the micro helped me cope with the macro, to dig deep on what really made me feel content — poems, the sound of rain, birdsong. I hope my piece talking back to Mary Oliver's poem inspires someone to return to the simple as well.

Contributing Youth Authors

Deandre Avant

Deandre is born and raised in Boston, Massachusetts. He went to Boston Arts Academy for five years as a Visual Arts Major. He now works for Teen Empower-ment as a Dancer and hopes to have his own dance studio for youth one day.

Genevieve Bascos-Arce

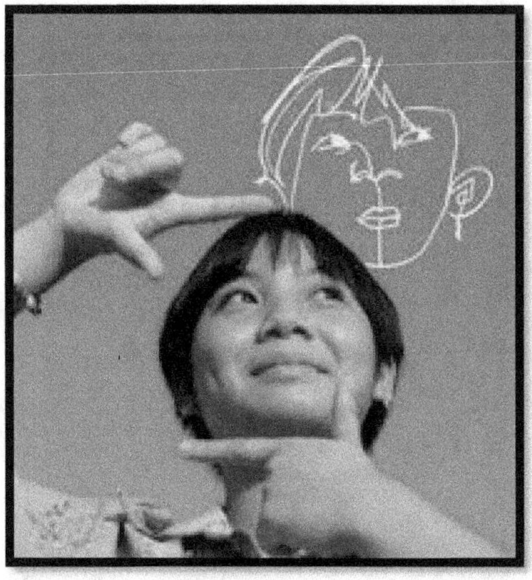

Genevieve is a Filipino-American freshman (14) studying at Dulles High School who hopes to showcase creativity in traditional careers such as medical science. She is looking forward to entering more creative writing work and art pieces to diverse platforms in the near future. Book after book and sketch after sketch, she enjoys reading fantasy and philosophy while working on paintings and sketches.

Niko Boskovic

Niko, age 20, lives in Portland, Oregon. He has dedicated himself to writing about life as a low-speaking autistic person. Niko finds that he is best able to express his lived experience through poetry, and has been published in Montana Mouthful; Lunch Ticket's Amuse-Bouche: Spotlight; In Parentheses Magazine; The Pointed Circle; and Kind Writers Magazine.

Keona Burch (Rose Zhāng)

Keona is from Portland, Oregon, but currently studying at Northfield Mount Hermon, a boarding high school in Massachusetts. She enjoys creative writing but only began writing poetry this past year. Since she has not had her work published before, she is so excited for this opportunity to share it. While she doesn't think she will pursue writing professionally in her future, she hopes to improve her writing and continue telling stories.

Ellenore "Ella" Celko

Ella is in the sixth grade at Childpeace Montessori School. She lives in Portland with her parents, brother, and two cats. She enjoys drawing and playing with her cats. She also loves sushi and macarons

Cara Chen

Cara is a student at Lakeridge High School. She has previously published work under the pen name Coco in the February 2022 and May 2022 editions of Tripping the Zine Fantastic, an online publication. She hopes to continue pursuing writing wholeheartedly, either as a hobby or a career, and she takes great joy in knowing that, somewhere out there, somebody is listening.

Katherine Elliott

Katherine is currently studying at Summit Olympus in the hopes of getting into college and becoming a Pharmacist. Previous work has included Creating a Story (Arts Corps) and various other art projects, so this is one of the first official works created. She hopes to continue creating stories and media to discover more possibilities in getting recognition for her work.

Trini Feng

Trini is a high school senior from suburban Illinois. Her work has previously been published in Hooligan Mag, Bluefire, and Ice Lolly Review, among others. She is also the Co-Editor-in-Chief of Renaissance Review, a literary journal that aims to bridge the gap between humanities and science by publishing interdisciplinary art and writing.

Journeya

Journeya resides in Mystic, Connecticut, with her soul companions: Callie the talkative cat, Jasper the energetic beagle, and all her wonderfully joyous plant friends. She is a writer, poet, an artist, and inconceivably ambitious. She spends her summers attending a program at Writer's Block Ink.

Danica Leung

A recent graduate from Lincoln High School, Danica intends to study political science at Emory University as a freshman in the fall. She has previously written for the Cardinal Times, and in Stepping Stone Publishing; she has also done freelance art work although this is first time publishing a graphic novel.

KyLynn Hattie Lucio

KyLynn is a junior at Springfield Public Schools in the hopes of becoming a therapist or a writer. This will be KyLynn's first time having her work published! She is extremely excited and she is so happy to be recognized for her work. She loves to write when she's feeling down so now she's happy to help others when they are feeling down!

Adrija Jana

Adrija is a passionately creative writer based in India. Apart from being a writer, Adrija is also a Spoken Word Artist, Theatrician, Filmmaker and creative researcher, and all her work is woven together by common themes. She believes that creative pieces that let the innate imperfection shine through truly touch hearts.

Mila Kashiwabara

Mila is so excited to be featured in this writing project. She is 10 years old and she lives in Portland Oregon. Mila is an actor, singer and dancer but in her free time she enjoys writing and journaling. This is her first writing piece that is going to be in an Ebook or be seen by people other than herself or her teachers.

Roodley Merilo

Roodley is a senior at New London High School who hopes to become an accomplished writer in the near future. Previous works have included writing *12 a.m. Thoughts* for Writer Block INC as well as being commissioned for a piece with F.R.E.S.H. In his free time, Roodley likes to take pictures for his community.

Erik Nielsen

Erik is an eleventh grader at Churchill High School and lives in Livonia, Michigan. While most of his time is devoted to school, he also loves to play basketball and enjoy the outdoors. He has recently realized the value of poetry as the ultimate form of expression.

Kaitlyn O'Neill

As a current high school student at Oregon Episcopal School, Kaitlyn discovered her love for poetry in her tenth-grade English class. Working with MediaRites is Kaitlyn's first professional project, but an adaptation of her poem was performed by Kaitlyn herself at the Armory in June 2022 with DanceAbility.

Veronica Salrin

Veronica is a sophomore at Center Grove High School in Greenwood, Indiana. This is their first time publishing, and they are beyond grateful for the opportunity. Veronica struggles with a connective tissue disorder and uses writing to describe their struggles in these areas. They hope to attend Rice University, Depaul University, or Carnegie Mellon to pursue a career in the design field or a social service field.

Isabella Santana

A recent graduate from West High School, Isabella hopes that her words can change the world. Isabella has received recognition for her writing on a local, state, and national level. She recently received the title of Los Angeles Youth Poet Ambassador, one of ten in Los Angeles County.
She felt elated when she saw her poem in print, and hopes to recreate that feeling of euphoria with a book of her own soon.

Freya Sticka

Freya is a 15 year old high schooler who lives in Portland Oregon. Freya loves to write, paint, and be creative. She is also very interested in learning Asian languages. She can speak Chinese Mandarin fluently. She is currently learning Japanese. Her goal is to attend Oxford University to study philosophy.

Jenell Theobald

Jenell Theobald is an incoming sophomore at the International School of Beaverton. She was born with developmental and physical disabilities, including high-functioning autism. She has done a lot of equity and advocacy work, including creating Let's Peer Up, a non-profit organization dedicated to supporting people with disabilities.

The –Ism Youth Files Creative Team

Dmae Roberts is the executive producer of MediaRites and is a veteran writer/producer who received two Peabody Awards for her documentary *Mei Mei, a Daughter's Song* and *Crossing East*, the first AAPI history series on public radio. She received the Dr. Suzanne Ahn Civil Rights and Social Justice award from the Asian American Journalists Association and is a USA Fellow and an Oregon Book Award winner. Her memoir book is *The Letting Go Trilogies: Stories of a Mixed-Race Family.* Through MediaRites, she also co-founded Theatre Diaspora, Oregon's first AAPI theater company. You can learn more about her at: **www.DmaeRoberts.com.**

Eleanor Gil-Kashiwabara, Psy.D. (she/her/ella) at Luminosa Psychological Services, LLC
Dr. Gil-Kashiwabara is a Licensed Psychologist based in Portland, OR. Her professional experience has focused on children and families experiencing a variety of issues including, but not limited to trauma, early childhood attachment disruptions and maltreatment, neurodevelopmental disorders and mood disorders. As a bilingual, Latinx psychologist, she is committed to providing culturally responsive services to all clients, while emphasizing the addressing of service inequities and culturally-specific service provision for communities of color. She founded *Luminosa Psychological Services*, which provides excellent training, consultation and supervision related to culturally responsive care, and equity, diversity and inclusion for providers, teachers, agencies, schools and organizations of all types including educational and arts organizations. You can learn more about her work at **www.LuminosaPsych.com.**

Samson Syharath is an actor, director, and writer focusing on visibility of Asian-American artists and underserved communities. Samson is the Managing Artistic Director of Theatre Diaspora, Associate Producer at MediaRites, part of the PDX Accountability Collective, and Board President of Portland Area Theatre Alliance.

Amanda Anderson (formerly Vander Hyde) is a freelance Stage and Production Manager, as well as Intimacy Choreographer, in the Portland area. She works as part of the Stage Management team at Portland Center Stage and Oregon Children's Theatre and is the Production Manager at MediaRites.

Sandra de Helen lives and writes in Portland, Oregon. In addition to being an accomplished editor, she is the author of over one hundred plays as well as: the Shirley Combs/Dr. Mary Watson mystery series, set in Portland; *Till Darkness Comes*, a thriller set in Kansas City, Missouri; and five collections of lesbian poetry published by Launch Point Press. de Helen is a member of the Golden Crown Literary Society, Dramatists Guild, Honor Roll! and International Centre for Women Playwrights. Follow her on Facebook at **www.facebook.com/SandradeHelenAuthor** or follow her on **Instagram @dehelen**.

Lori L. Lake is an author, teacher, editor, and jack of all trades when it comes to publishing. She runs a small publishing house, Train Wreck XPress, and enjoys cover creation, typesetting, and formatting ebooks. Over the last two-plus decades, she has written seventeen books including crime fiction, romances, short stories, a historical novel of World War II, and four anthologies for which she served as editor. You can find out more about Lori at: **www.LoriLLake.com**.

Thanks to Our Supporters

The –Ism Youth Files book and podcast project
received support from:

Ronni Lacroute
The Regional Arts And Culture Council
Oregon Community Foundation
James F. and Marion L. Miller Foundation
Oregon Arts Commission
Collins Foundation
Oregon Humanities
Miller Foundation
WESTAF
The City of Portland Arts Healing grant,
and thank you to all the individual donors.

Thank you to Oregon Children's Theatre for partnering with MediaRites on The Youth Mental Health Toolkit as part of this project. Get a free download of the toolkit at **MediaRites.org** where you can also hear our *The –Ism Youth Files* podcast.

MediaRites Staff

Dmae Lo Roberts, executive producer
Samson Syharath, associate producer
Amanda Anderson, production manager

MediaRites Board

Sara Caswell Kolbet, president
Larry Toda, secretary
Tara Gatewood
Shelley B. Shelley
Clark Salisbury
Sandra de Helen
Dmae Lo Roberts

MediaRites is a tax-exempt, 501 (c) 3, nonprofit production organization based in Portland, Oregon, dedicated to telling the stories of diverse cultures and giving voice to the unheard through the arts, education, and media projects.

Find out more about MediaRites at:

www.MediaRites.org

Copyright Permissions

A Quarantine Poem (or The Best Ways to Dull the Ache in My Boredom) © 2023 Niko Boskovic, printed with permission of author.

A Wish for Rain © 2023 Keona Burch, printed with permission of author.

Bent and Broken © 2023 Veronica Salrin, printed with permission of author.

Consequence of Culture © 2023 Genevieve Bascos-Arce, graphic artwork and story printed with permission of author/artist.

*COVID: We Went Through that S**t* © 2023 Journeya, printed with permission of author.

During and Now © 2023 Journeya, printed with permission of author.

Fault © 2023 Keona Burch, printed with permission of author.

"Foreword" © 2023 Dmae Lo Roberts, printed with permission of author.

Good Kid © 2023 Danica Leung, graphic artwork and story printed with permission of author/artist.

Home • sick • ness © 2023 Cara Chen, printed with permission of author.

How We Speak Our Truths © 2023 Trini Feng, printed with permission of author.

"Introduction" © 2023 Eleanor Gil-Kashiwabara, printed with permission of author.

Loosen the Ties Which Bind Us to This Place © 2023 Niko Boskovic, printed with permission of author.

Lost © 2023 Erik Nielsen, printed with permission of author.